DAILY
GUIDEPOSTS
Journeys

35 YEARS OF AMERICA'S BEST-LOVED DEVOTIONAL

Guideposts
New York, New York

Daily Guideposts Journeys

ISBN-13: 978-0-8249-4829-0

Published by Guideposts
16 East 34th Street
New York, New York 10016
www.guideposts.com

Distributed by Ideals Publications, a Guideposts company
2630 Elm Hill Pike, Suite 100
Nashville, Tennessee 37214

Acknowledgments

Every attempt has been made to credit the sources of copyrighted material used in this book. If any such acknowledgment has been inadvertently omitted or miscredited, receipt of such information would be appreciated.

Scripture quotations marked (NAS) are taken from the *New American Standard Bible*, copyright © 1960, 1962, 1963, 1968, 1971, 1972, 1973, 1975, 1977, 1995 by the Lockman Foundation. Used by permission.

Scripture quotations marked (NEB) are taken from *The New English Bible*. Copyright © The Delegates of the Oxford University Press and the Syndics of the Cambridge University Press 1961, 1970.

Scripture quotations marked (NIV) are taken from *The Holy Bible, New International Version*. Copyright © 1973, 1978, 1984 International Bible Society. Used by permission of Zondervan Bible Publishers.

Scripture quotations marked (NKJV) are taken from *The Holy Bible, New King James Version*. Copyright © 1997, 1990, 1985, 1983 by Thomas Nelson, Inc.

Scripture quotations marked (NLT) are taken from the *Holy Bible*, New Living Translation. Copyright © 1996. Used by permission of Tyndale House Publishers, Inc., Wheaton, Illinois 60189. All rights reserved.

Scripture quotations marked (RSV) are taken from the *Revised Standard Version of the Bible*. Copyright © 1946, 1952, 1971 by Division of Christian Education of the National Council of Churches of Christ in the U.S.A. Used by permission.

Scripture quotations marked (TLB) are taken from *The Living Bible*. Copyright © 1971 by Tyndale House Publishers, Wheaton, Illinois 60187. All rights reserved.

Cover design by Faceout Studio
Cover photo by iStock
Interior design by Gretchen Schuler-Dandridge
Typeset by Aptara

Printed and bound in the United States of America
10 9 8 7 6 5 4 3 2 1

Contents

2010

2011

Introduction

Thirty-five years ago, a book was born. Its purpose was to provide the readers of *Guideposts* with a daily source of the kind of spirit-lifting messages they read monthly in the magazine and with the tools to develop, as the flap copy put it, "an every day habit of devotion." That first edition, *Daily Guideposts*, 1977, surprised everyone by selling 189,000 copies; since then, more than twenty million copies of *Daily Guideposts* have been sold.

The format has varied little since 1977: For every day of the year, *Daily Guideposts* offers a short, first-person story, preceded by a quotation (now always a Scripture) verse and concluded with a prayer. But within those constraints, our writers have provided readers with insight into the presence of God in our everyday lives, pointed out ways to a richer prayer life, given contemporary context to the Scriptures and, perhaps most importantly, opened their hearts and their lives to their readers. And so something remarkable has happened: A family has been born, a remarkable family of readers and writers—some of whom have been with us for more than thirty years—united by a deep sharing of their joys and sorrows, hopes and fears, by their prayers for each other and by their faith in the God Who accompanies them every day of their lives.

This book contains what we feel is the best of *Daily Guideposts*. In its more than one hundred devotionals, we've tried to represent the full range of writers and subjects that have appeared in our pages. We've named this book *Daily Guideposts Journeys* because we want to give you a glimpse of the journeys our writers have taken over these thirty-five years. And to help you remember your own journey, we've included some of the events that have changed our world and a few of the books, films and music that have shaped our sensibilities through the last quarter of the twentieth century and the first decade of the twenty-first. If you're a *Daily Guideposts* reader, we hope this book brings back some memories. If you're not, we hope that what you find here will encourage you to join our family for the journeys yet to come.

Andrew Attaway
Editor, *Daily Guideposts*

1977

A revolution began in 1977 that would transform the way we do our jobs, keep up with each other, and inform and entertain ourselves. In January of that year, the first personal computer, the Commodore PET, was demonstrated at a consumer electronics show in Chicago, and a new company, Apple Computer, was incorporated. Other new beginnings came that year, as well: Jimmy Carter became the 39th president of the United States, while Deng Xiaoping expelled the "Gang of Four" from power in China. We were reading *The Thorn Birds* and *The Book of Lists* and listening again to Elvis Presley as we mourned his sudden death. When the miniseries *Roots* didn't have us riveted to the TV set, *Star Wars* had us crowding into the movie theaters. It cost us thirteen cents to mail a first-class letter.

That was the world into which *Daily Guideposts* was born, the product of one man's determination to make a colleague's dream come true. We'll let that man, Fred Bauer, tell the story in his own words:

In the Beginning

The roots of *Daily Guideposts* go back to 1962, and perhaps before. But 1962 is when I came on the scene as an editor for *Guideposts* magazine.

Once or twice a month, the *Guideposts* staff—full-time and part-time editors and writers—gathered around a big conference table on the sixth floor of a building right behind Marble Collegiate Church at Fifth Avenue and 29th Street to review upcoming articles and make plans for future projects. I can remember showing up for my first meeting full of trepidation and jitters, in awe of the talent around that table. Almost all those gathered were accomplished magazine writers and authors—the Peales, Len LeSourd, John and Elizabeth Sherrill, Catherine Marshall, Arthur Gordon, Van Varner, Sidney Fields, Glenn Kittler.

There isn't much I remember about that meeting, except that Len mentioned his hope that someday Guideposts would be able to produce "an inspiring daily book of readings, full of deep spiritual takeaways" like the then-twenty-four-page, two-color magazine. All agreed it was a worthwhile idea but that "it would be a long time before we'd have the manpower to do it." (I'm sure we said "manpower" back then.)

They were right—it did take a long time. Thirteen years later we were still talking about a daily devotional, and we still didn't have enough writers to launch such a book. But one day during the summer of 1975, while on vacation, I got to thinking about a Guideposts devotional. Was it a lack of people that kept us from producing such a book, I wondered, or a lack of vision?

Maybe I could get the project rolling. I decided to draft a month of devotionals to see how long it would take. For several weeks I experimented, trying to create something fresh and vital. It was slow going. Unless the readings were lively and helpful, I felt, there was no need to continue.

There had to be a daily nugget of Scripture and a prayer, I knew. And the stories and illustrations needed to be applicable to daily life, faith-building, uplifting, positive, encouraging. *Don't sermonize or present homilies*, a still, small voice whispered, *but you should draw on the power and authority of God's Word*.

When my vacation was over, I carried the twenty-five or thirty devotionals I'd written into the office to show the staff. The Peales and editor Arthur Gordon were enthusiastic but were probably doubtful that I could write the whole book.

I was executive editor by then, doubling as book editor, and certainly didn't need anything more to do, but because I believed such a book could be helpful, I was determined to write it. We did a reader survey that indicated there was interest in a devotional, so I began writing furiously toward a September 1976 deadline. With the help of many others and lots of answered prayers, I finished 365 devotionals in time and *Daily Guideposts, 1977* was offered to our subscribers. In just a couple of weeks, it was clear we would have to go back to press. Orders exceeded our expectations.

I wrote *Daily Guideposts, 1978*, too, before calling in reinforcements. And the multivoiced books that followed my first two volumes have continued to find an appreciative audience into a new century. When I'm asked why I think *Daily Guideposts* has flourished, I tell people it's because we followed Dr. Peale's old formula for success: Find a need and fill it. And one other reason: The editors and writers have faithfully produced what Len LeSourd envisioned way back in 1962: "an inspiring daily book of readings, full of deep spiritual takeaways."

A journalist, editor, biographer, poet, storyteller and, above all, consummate professional, overflowing with creative ideas and fascinating facts from history, the arts, sports and his own extensive travels, Fred could also tell a tender family story or a touching personal anecdote, as in the following story about his Grandmother Bauer.

Grandmother's Lilies

He's the lily of the valley,
The bright and morning star,
He's the fairest of ten thousand to my soul....
—GOSPEL HYMN

My Grandmother Bauer has been dead for thirty years, but last summer at the lake cottage that she loved so much, her white lilies, planted six decades ago, bloomed once again, as gorgeous as ever. Whenever I look at those perennial flowers, I am warmed by the memory of her. They are a symbol of her life.

Christians have many symbols—the fish, the cup, the bread, the star, the manger—but the most important one is the cross, because it is the crucial symbol of our faith. It reminds us of Christ's sacrifice, which assures everlasting life to all who believe in Him. Each summer when I journey several hundred miles to my boyhood haunt, I expectantly look for Grandmother's lilies, hoping to find them blooming once more. So far they have never failed. In a small way, those resilient flowers reflect the hope of my faith, the hope and the promise that transcends the grave....

Though the grass withers and the flowers fade, Lord,
I know Your Word shall stand forever.
—FRED BAUER, JULY 20, 1977

1978

Peace and popes dominated the headlines in 1978: Egypt's Anwar Sadat and Israel's Menachem Begin signed the Camp David Accord, for which they would receive the Nobel Prize, while in Rome the death of Pope Paul VI was followed by the thirty-four-day reign of John Paul I and the beginning of the very long pontificate of John Paul II, the first Polish pope.

Garfield the cat made his debut on the comics page of our newspapers, while we picked up Robert Ludlum's *Holcroft Convention,* James Michener's *Chesapeake,* Herman Wouk's *War and Remembrance,* James Fixx's *Complete Book of Running* and Erma Bombeck's *If Life Is a Bowl of Cherries, What Am I Doing in the Pits?* on our visits to the bookstore. *The Deer Hunter* and *Coming Home* brought a post-Vietnam war soberness to the movie theaters, while we laughed at *Heaven Can Wait.* We listened to "I Will Survive" by Gloria Gaynor and "Roxanne" by the Police on our brand-new Sony Walkman portable stereos. Prices were rising, and by the end of May, a first-class stamp cost fifteen cents.

Fred Bauer was still the writer of all 365 *Daily Guideposts* devotionals. The selection that follows shows how Fred could use a telling quote or an interesting story to make a devotional point.

The Uses of Adversity

"Jesus said unto him, "If thou canst believe, all things are
possible to him that believeth."

—MARK 9:23

As a young man, I attended many baseball games at Detroit's Briggs Stadium, and though Ty Cobb had long before retired, his legend was very much alive. At one time he held more hitting and base-stealing records than any player in the game. But the statistics don't reveal his greatest asset: a never-say-die, competitive spirit.

When I think of Ty Cobb, I am reminded that his baseball career almost died aborning. In his first season, he played in only forty-one games for the Augusta, Georgia, team and hit a measly .237. The management saw no great talent in him and told him he was through.

Cobb was discouraged and wrote of those feelings in a letter to his father. The elder Cobb was unsympathetic in his curt reply. The essence of it was: "Don't come home until you've given it your all."

Ty Cobb took his dad's advice. He got another job in baseball, and the following year drew raves wherever he played. In a few short years, he was the most heralded player in the major leagues. Eventually, he was enshrined in baseball's Hall of Fame.

When you face setbacks and think there is no hope, be careful not to give up too soon. Many a success story has been built on a foundation of early frustration and failure. "Sweet are the uses of adversity," wrote Shakespeare, and he was right. Out of ashes came the phoenix. Out of darkness God made light. Out of clay He shaped man. And out of a borrowed tomb came the Savior of the world.

When our hopes resemble dying embers, Lord,
fan them with Your love.
—FRED BAUER, JUNE 5, 1978

1979

Regime change was in the air and in the headlines in 1979. Forces backed by Vietnam overthrew the almost unbelievably brutal regime of Pol Pot in Cambodia, and the Ayatollah Khomeini's Islamic Revolution swept the Shah off the throne of Iran. Cold War fears eased as President Carter and Soviet President Brezhnev signed the second strategic arms limitation treaty, while other fears grew as the Three Mile Island nuclear reactor in Pennsylvania released radiation. And in London, Louise Brown, the world's first test-tube baby, was born, a sign of hope for some and a cause of disquiet for others.

Some familiar names dominated book sales (Arthur Hailey with *Overload*, Stephen King with *The Dead Zone*, Robert Ludlum with *The Matarese Circle*, William Styron with *Sophie's Choice*, Erma Bombeck's *Aunt Erma's Cope Book*) along with some less familiar (Wil Huygen and Rien Poortvlet with *Gnomes* and Dr. Herman Tarnower and Samm Sinclair Baker with *The Complete Scarsdale Medical Diet*). In the theaters we watched *Apocalypse Now, All That Jazz, Kramer vs. Kramer* and *Breaking Away,* while Pink Floyd's "Another Brick in the Wall, Part 2," "London Calling" by the Clash and "Rapper's Delight"—the first commercial rap—by the Sugarhill Gang were on the charts. A first-class stamp was still fifteen cents.

But if the price of postage was holding steady, that wasn't the case with *Daily Guideposts.* We experienced a quantum jump—from one writer to seventy-five, including such standouts as Dr. and Mrs. Norman Vincent Peale, Marjorie Holmes and Catherine Marshall. A number of writers who joined our family in 1979 are still with us, including Elizabeth and John Sherrill, Marion Bond West, Marilyn Morgan Helleberg, Isabel Champ (Wolseley), and Penney Schwab. And in addition to writers, we added features to our devotional: "Your Spiritual Workshop," a monthly series that echoed a popular feature in *Guideposts* magazine, and our first Holy Week series.

We've chosen three very different writers to represent that year. Eleanor Sass, a longtime editor at *Guideposts* magazine, was deaf, and so was her mother. Here she tells how her mother taught her that, no matter what our limitations, God has opportunities in store for all of us.

Natural-born writers can be found on every level of the *Guideposts* staff, and Naomi Lawrence, executive secretary to several editors-in-chief, was no exception. A widow from Brooklyn, New York, she learned from the best how to write an inspirational story. In her devotional, she tells us about a moment her mother remembered—and Naomi would never forget.

Zona B. Davis of Effingham, Illinois, wrote of many things during her eight years with *Daily Guideposts*—the beauty of nature, her husband Plaford, her son Paul, her grandchildren, her travels—and here about a sign of faith we pass through our fingers every day.

The Open Door

*When one door closes, another opens but we often look so long
and so regretfully upon the closed door that we do not see
the one which has opened for us.*
—ALEXANDER GRAHAM BELL

s a child, Evelyn Sass had a promising singing voice and was often called upon to sing the solo parts in church and school productions. With her teacher's encouragement, she began to dream of a musical career.

Then, suddenly, in her early teens, through a series of illnesses, Evelyn lost her hearing totally. The dream of becoming a singer died. She became depressed and withdrawn, spending long hours alone, until one day her teacher came to visit.

"You know, Evelyn," the teacher said, "God gave us five senses. You still have four of them. I challenge you to concentrate on one of these. See if you can't develop it beyond the norm so that what you gain in one offsets the loss in another."

Evelyn did. She chose sight, and she worked and worked at it until she had developed such a remarkable skill at lipreading that in 1930 she won the National Lipreading Tournament held in New York City. In addition she went on to have a successful business career, married and bore a daughter—me.

I'm proud of my mother—and I know what she went through because I also have a hearing problem and rely on lipreading. And like my mother I have come to know that there are many doors in this life. What a waste of time it is to keep on staring at a door you know cannot be opened. And how exciting it is to find the one that God swings wide for you!

Father, thank You for opening my eyes to the thrilling opportunities You set before us.
—ELEANOR SASS, MARCH 6, 1979

A Birthday Miracle

I would be true, for there are those who trust me.
—HOWARD ARNOLD WALTER

*M*y mother always loved lilacs. From the time I was old enough to save my pennies for her birthday, she always had lilacs on May 11. Then, in her last year, after a long, downhill period of suffering, her mind wandered; she didn't remember where she was or who I was. So when May 11 came around I thought, *Why bother? She hasn't responded to anything for days now.* But tradition prevailed, and I arrived at the hospital with a small spray of her beloved blossoms. As I arranged them in the vase on the bedside table, standing with my back to Mom's bed, a voice came forth clearly from behind me. "How lovely. It's my birthday. You didn't forget."

For that one brief moment, just two weeks before she died, Mom came back for one last visit.

Thank You, Lord, for this tiny miracle that never lets me forget to honor the living while they are alive.
—NAOMI LAWRENCE, MAY 11, 1979

"In God We Trust"

I pledge allegiance to the flag of the United States...
one nation, under God. ...
—FRANCIS BELLAMY

*W*orried about Union defeats at Fort Sumter and Bull Run and concerned about the godlessness of a nation that set brother against brother in a civil war, The Reverend Mr. Watkinson, Protestant minister of Ridleyville, Pennsylvania, decided to do something in the name of God.

On a November day in 1861, he wrote to Treasury Secretary Salmon P. Chase. "One fact touching our currency has hitherto been seriously overlooked," he said. "I mean the recognition of the Almighty God in some form on our coins. What if our Republic were now shattered beyond reconstruction? Would not the antiquaries of succeeding centuries rightly reason from our past that we were a heathen nation?"

As a result, Philadelphia mint director James Pollock was ordered to prepare a motto expressing the nation's recognition of its dependency upon God.

In 1864 the inscription "In God We Trust" first appeared on a US coin—the two-cent piece. After 1864 the phrase appeared on many coins, but only since 1938, with coinage of the Jefferson nickel, have all US coins carried this inscription.

Isn't it heartening to think that every day millions of Americans carry in their pockets this quiet affirmation of the nation's allegiance to God?

Lord, how great it is to put our trust in You.
—ZONA B. DAVIS, NOVEMBER 14, 1979

1980

The aftermath of the Iranian revolution brought the seizure of the US embassy in November 1979, and the ensuing crisis dominated the news this year. And we could get that news in a new way: CNN debuted as the first all-news network. In reaction to the Soviet invasion of Afghanistan, the United States boycotted the 1980 Moscow Olympics. Ronald Reagan was elected to his first term as president, while in December, former Beatle John Lennon was murdered outside his Manhattan apartment building.

Raging Bull, Ordinary People, Coal Miner's Daughter and *The Elephant Man* were hits at the box office; *Smiley's People* by John le Carré, *Princess Daisy* by Judith Krantz, *The Bourne Identity* by Robert Ludlum, *Rage of Angels* by Sidney Sheldon, *Firestarter* by Stephen King, *Key to Rebecca* by Ken Follett and *The Covenant* by James Michener were hits in the bookstores; Bette Midler sang about "The

Rose" and Willie Nelson was "On the Road Again." First-class postage continued to hold at fifteen cents.

We welcomed seventy-three writers to *Daily Guideposts, 1980.* Among them were three first-timers destined to become reader favorites: Oscar Greene, a beloved presence in all but four editions of *Daily Guideposts* since his debut, Shari Smyth and Sue Monk Kidd, who has gone on to become one of America's most noted novelists. And that year saw another notable first: our first paperback large-print edition.

Marion Bond West, the author of the first of our 1980 devotionals, contended with the illness and death of her first husband, the difficulties of being a single mother and a sometimes quick temper. But she faced it all with indomitable faith and a humble heart and shared it with her readers with unflinching honesty. Here she shares a tender moment with one of her twin sons—and her heavenly Father.

Sue Monk Kidd was born and raised in Sylvester, Georgia. She studied nursing at Texas Christian University, where she met her husband-to-be Sandy. After their marriage, Sue and Sandy lived in Georgia, served as missionaries in Africa, and then settled down in South Carolina. In 1978, Sue went to the Guideposts Writers Workshop and published her first *Guideposts* article in 1979. In this devotional from her 1980 *Daily Guideposts* debut, she uses a simple but profound metaphor to describe the stresses and strains of mother's life—and the way through them.

Catherine Marshall was one of the best-loved and most prolific inspirational writers of the first half of the twentieth century. She was married to Peter Marshall, a poor Scottish immigrant who became a renowned preacher and was twice the chaplain of the US Senate; her book about him, *A Man Called Peter,* written after his untimely death at age forty-six, became a best seller, as did her novels *Christy* and *Julie.* The stories about her childhood that were retold in her fiction also found their way into her devotionals, as in this story of her mother's secret for abundant living.

Just a Little Thing

Giving thanks always for all things unto God and the Father
in the name of our Lord Jesus Christ.
—EPHESIANS 5:20

One cold night I stopped by my twin sons' room to check on them before going to bed. They both appeared to be asleep. However, Jon murmured, "Cold, Mama." Checking in their closet, I couldn't find a blanket, so I slipped off my bathrobe and covered Jon with it. In the moonlight that came in through the window, I carefully tucked it under his feet and chin. He was so still and quiet, I was sure he was asleep.

The boys were nearly eleven and I didn't often tuck them in at night. I went on down the dark hall to my bed and climbed in wearily. It had been a long, hard day. I knew I'd be asleep within minutes.

"Mama," came the call from the boys' room. I sighed, hoping Jon didn't need anything else.

"Yes?"

In a tone soft for Jon, he said, "It was nice when you took off your robe and gave it to me and even tucked me in. Thanks."

The unexpected thanks from my son touched my heart and then caused me to smile in the darkness. My boys seldom expressed gratitude. I was always after them to say thank you.

"You're welcome," I answered. "'Night. Sweet dreams," I added happily.

And then I didn't go right to sleep. Instead, I thought about how Jon's thanking me for such a little thing had pleased me. Prompted by his gratitude, I began to thank my Father for many little things I'd neglected to say thanks for through the day.

Father, God, thank You, thank You, thank You.
—MARION BOND WEST, FEBRUARY 7, 1980

A Dry-Cup Day

Fill my cup. Lord, I lift it up. Lord. . . .
—RICHARD BLANCHARD

I was a wreck! My son had driven a grocery cart through the cake-mix display at the supermarket, my daughter had bathed eight stuffed animals in a tub of water, and the dog had turned over three newly potted geraniums on the rug. I could go on, but I won't depress you. I was having one of my dry-cup days.

I get them. Maybe you do too. They are the days that leave me empty as a dry cup. You know the ones—ringing phones, children's quarrels, spilled grape juice, overdue library books, and a frantic tangle of errands and demands. All together these little frustrations can wear a hole in my day through which peace and perspective drain away.

You know what I did? I dropped everything and carried my dry cup to an armchair in the bedroom. Hidden away from the distractions, I closed my eyes and held up my cup to God for a refill. I didn't think of the forty boxes of cake mix crashing down or the waterlogged animals or the carpet full of potting soil. I thought about God. I imagined Him pouring down His love and peace and strength upon me. There, in those few silent moments, He filled my cup. Filled it up. And I returned to the little human things of life, my cup brimming with peace.

On the dry-cup days, Lord, help me to seek
a quiet corner for a refill.
—SUE MONK KIDD, FEBRUARY 21, 1980

Mother's Secret

Not what we give, but what we share,
For the gift without the giver is bare;
Who gives himself with his alms feeds three,
Himself, his hungering neighbor, and me.
—JAMES RUSSELL LOWELL

*I*n the small West Virginia town where I grew up, the Depression seemed to strike especially hard. My father was a minister, and since most people in his church suffered such financial setbacks, he voluntarily accepted three successive cuts in salary. Our family of five barely scraped along. Yet we never knew desperation or fear because of my mother's secret for an abundant life.

In those days we rarely could afford meat, and our pantry was always slimly stocked, yet Mother's custard was velvety smooth, her rolls feather-light, and her corn mush legendary. Sliced thin, browned crisply and served with maple syrup on our best china, the mush Mother made was always an occasion.

Somehow she learned that Mr. Edwards, our wealthy neighbor, loved mush, but never got it because his wife thought it lowly fare.

So from time to time Mother would send us children over to the Edwards house with hot, fresh, golden-fried mush. "Poor Mister Edwards," we'd say as we hurried it over to him-and not be kidding.

And that was the core of Mother's secret. How can a family be wanting, if it is giving things away?

> *Lord, keep reminding me that it is only when I give that*
> *I am truly participating in Your abundance.*
> —CATHERINE MARSHALL, AUGUST 28, 1980

1981

The world was shocked in 1981 when Egyptian president and Nobel Prizewinner Anwar Sadat was assassinated by Islamic extremists. In the US, Sandra Day O'Connor became the first woman justice on the Supreme Court, and the Major League Baseball season was interrupted by a strike. Many of us got up extra early on a July Wednesday to watch the fairy-tale spectacle of the wedding of Prince Charles and Princess Diana.

The best sellers we read that year included *Gorky Park* by Martin Cruz Smith, *Noble House* by James Clavell, *Cujo* by Stephen King, *The Hotel New Hampshire* by John Irving, *An Indecent Obsession* by Colleen McCullough and James Herriot's *The Good Lord Made Them All*. We tapped our toes to Kim Carnes's "Bette Davis Eyes," "For Your Eyes Only" by Sheena Easton, "Breakin' Away" by Al Jarreau, "Jesse's Girl" by Rick Springfield, Pat Benatar's "Fire and Ice" and the theme from the new hit TV series *Hill Street Blues*. At the movies, we marveled at the first Indiana Jones adventure, *Raiders of the Lost Ark,* found a genuine hero of faith in *Chariots of Fire,* and shed a tear *On Golden Pond* with Katherine Hepburn and Henry Fonda. Our postage took a big jump, from fifteen cents to eighteen cents as of March 22 and to twenty cents as of November 1.

Our *Daily Guideposts* family also took a jump that year, to an awesome and never-equaled ninety-eight contributors, including newcomers Karen Barber, Aletha J. Lindstrom and Mary Jane Meyer. We packed in the features too: "When the Bible Speaks to Me" in the middle of each month, "A Lenten Visit with Norman Vincent Peale" and a Holy Week series by Sue Monk Kidd.

We've chosen three writers to represent 1981: Patricia Houck Sprinkle of Oak Park, Illinois, appeared in *Daily Guideposts* from 1979 to 1986. As a mother, a minister's wife and a writer, Patricia had her hands full with the chores and concerns of daily life, as well as with a writer's deadlines. But, as her 1981 devotional shows, her bulging to-do list never kept her from looking up—in gratitude. Dee Anne Palmer of Redlands, California, was an experienced, caring nurse who was part of our family from 1980 to 1982. But as you'll see, even Dee Anne had to learn to value compassion over correctness. The writer of our third selection, Doris Haase of Sherman Oaks, California, got up at 5:00 AM every day to pray, study the Bible and read a devotional. Ever active, she swam, biked, walked, and attended movies and plays. So on Mother's Day, she wasn't about to meekly sit back and wait for an invitation to find her.

A Friend in the Sky

When I consider Thy heavens, the work of Thy fingers,
the moon and the stars, which Thou hast ordained.
—PSALM 8:3

I have always loved the stars. When I was a child, my daddy would come into our room on cold crisp nights, wrap my sister and me up in a quilt and carry us out under the clear sky. Then he would point out the constellations and tell us their stories.

My favorite was Orion, the mighty hunter with his three-star belt and his faithful dog. Even now I await his arrival each fall with the eagerness of childhood, and search for him in winter skies.

Last fall we moved 1,500 miles to an unfamiliar city. One evening I found myself unbearably homesick—so homesick I yearned not only for the city we had just left, but for all the homes I had ever known. As I stood on my back porch and poured out my loneliness to God, I suddenly saw my old friend Orion climbing over the horizon.

"Here I am!" he seemed to say. "Did you think you'd left me behind too? I've just come from those you love far to the east, and I go to those you love in the west. Does the world seem big to you tonight? I shall visit it all before dawn. Are you anxious about tomorrow and what it will bring? Don't be afraid, little one. The God Who made you made me eons before, and He holds tomorrow in His hand."

Watching Orion's confident climb into the sky, I found my heart gently eased. Once more the whole earth was "home," the household and family of God.

Dear Lord, thank You for the heavens that remind us that
You hold the universe in Your mighty hand.
—PATRICIA HOUCK SPRINKLE, JANUARY 9, 1981

The Piano Tuner

A friend loveth at all times, and a brother is born for adversity.
—PROVERBS 17:17

Mr. Witchel was eighty and, because of his experience, charged a high fee to tune our piano. My husband and I would have paid it gladly, but the upper octaves of our piano still sounded like sour lemons.

We complained and Mr. Witchel reworked it. It wasn't any better. In fact, he denied that anything was wrong. But to placate us, he agreed to bring another tuner for a second opinion.

The second tuner, a man of fifty, agreed with Mr. Witchel that the piano was perfect. Suspecting collaboration, we angrily ordered them out of the house.

Half an hour later, the second tuner returned, bag in hand.

"You're right about those high notes," he admitted. "But you see, Elmer's hearing is going." He shook his head sadly. "He taught me how to tune pianos and for sixty years he has lived for tuning. I just can't tell this man, my friend, that his life is over."

He corrected the tuning for free, asking us to keep it a secret.

Elmer Witchel is gone now, so he can't be hurt if I share this story. I think of him often, and of his friend too, knowing this is the kind of love Jesus wants me to show: a love that preserves the dignity of a friend.

I need a touch of Your sensitivity, Lord,
to be a true and faithful friend.
—DEE ANNE PALMER, MARCH 26, 1981

A Mother's Day Sermon

There is more pleasure in loving than in being loved.
—THOMAS FULLER

I sat looking out the church window. It was Mother's Day and I hadn't heard from my son. *He's forgotten,* I thought, shifting uneasily in my seat. Of course my son and his wife have a very busy life. They are preoccupied. Still...disappointment settled around me like fog as I listened to the minister's sermon.

"Mother's Day is a time of love," he declared. "Don't let the day pass without saying 'I love you'—children to your mothers, and mothers to your children."

Mothers to your children. I sat up straighter. *Why not? Why couldn't I be the one to call?*

I picked up the telephone the moment I got home.

"Gary," I cried eagerly, "I'm coming over to take you both out for a Mother's Day supper. I want to celebrate the wonderful children God gave me."

"Hey, Mom, I'm glad you called," he answered. "We've been trying to reach you. We've already made reservations!"

My depression was gone. That day turned out to be one of the happiest days I've ever had.

Lord, help me remember that I can never feel sorry for myself
when I am busy loving.
—DORIS HAASE, MAY 10, 1981

1982

The year 1982 saw the failure of the Equal Rights Amendment to be ratified as an amendment to the US Constitution. Dr. Barney Clark became the first person to receive an implanted artificial heart, and Princess Grace of Monaco, the former film star Grace Kelly, died of injuries she sustained in an auto accident.

On the shelves at our bookstores were *North and South* by John Jakes, *The Parsifal Mosaic* by Robert Ludlum, *The Prodigal Daughter* by Jeffrey Archer, *Different Seasons* by Stephen King, *Space* by James Michener, and *A Few Minutes with Andy Rooney*. In the movie theaters, we were watching *E.T.: The Extra-Terrestrial*, *Tootsie*, *Gandhi* and *The Verdict*; while "Rosanna" by Toto, "Always on My Mind" by Willie Nelson, "Eye of the Tiger" by Survivor, "Age to Age" by Amy Grant and "Higher Plane" by Al Green were on our radios. And for the first time, we could listen to our music on compact discs. The cost of a first-class stamp was steady at twenty cents.

Seventy-nine writers graced *Daily Guideposts, 1982*. We featured a new series of "When the Bible Speaks to Me" devotionals, as well as our first Advent series and a special three-page Christmas story by Dr. Peale. We welcomed Madge Harrah, a longtime friend, as a new member of the clan.

The redoubtable Marjorie Holmes had a unique ability to speak to people, particularly women, going through difficult times. Though she's perhaps best remembered for her novel *Two from Galilee*, her *I've Got to Talk to Somebody, God* brought a simple, conversational style of prayer into the homes and hearts of people all over America. Left a widow after forty-seven years of marriage, she prayed, "God, send me a wonderful man." And He did—George Schmieler, a widower who had read her books and was determined to meet her. She wrote about their life together in *Second Wife, Second Life* and in the devotionals she contributed during her twenty-two years with *Daily Guideposts*.

Richard Schneider, a fixture at Guideposts for thirty-eight years, could turn out a beautifully crafted story on his old manual typewriter at the drop of a deadline. Dick could take a magazine story idea that perplexed others and spin it into gold. And as you'll see, he was no less proficient with devotionals.

Our third devotional comes from Sue Monk Kidd, a beautifully crafted memory of a long-ago day, a wise old woman and an unforgettable lesson in giving.

Talking to the Father

Dear Lord and Father of mankind. . . .
—JOHN G. WHITTIER

*O*ur Father Who art in heaven. . . . To most of us, these words seem absolutely true and natural. They state so clearly our relation to God. But when my friend Bilquis Sheikh became a Christian, those words troubled her.

Born in Pakistan, Bilquis grew up believing that God was a distant and impersonal power. Even when she later came to know and love Jesus Christ, she still couldn't believe that God was someone she could think of as her father.

Trying to help Bilquis, a friend said, "Talk to God in the same way you always talked to your father, your dad."

This technique didn't work right away, but it got Bilquis thinking of her father. "When I was a little girl," she told me, "and would have to ask my father something, I was at first afraid. He worked in an office at home and I'd peek in, not wanting to interrupt. When he saw me, though, he'd put down his pen and call out his pet name for me.

'Keecha,' he'd say, 'come, my darling.' Then he'd put his arm around me and ask me about my troubles."

The more Bilquis thought of these fatherly moments, the more she saw that being a father meant always listening lovingly to a troubled child.

Kneeling in her room, now a grown-up woman, Bilquis looked up to heaven and cried out, "Oh, Father, Father God." And as she prayed, a wonderful warmth filled her. That warmth told her that God is our Father, always listening for us.

Our Father, my Father, Who art in heaven . . .
—RICHARD SCHNEIDER, AUGUST 8, 1982

After the Storm

*A new heart also will I give you, and a new spirit will
I put within you...*
—EZEKIEL 36:26

The summer that hurricane Agnes struck our area in Virginia my husband and I were on a trip west. Phone calls warned us that the flood had swept through the lower floor of our summer home on Lake Jackson. "And all those beautiful roses you set out are gone!"

It was a sorry sight to which we returned. Inside—mud, ruined furniture, water-soaked books, papers, clothes. Outside—stone walls collapsed, tress uprooted, the float torn free and leaning drunkenly halfway up the opposite bank. Heartsick, we plunged into cleaning up the mess. But as we worked, aided by wonderful neighbors, we heard the stories of devastation elsewhere. Even so, we could hardly bear to look toward that ravished rose garden.

Bald in places, buried by debris in others, it looked utterly hopeless. "It's pretty late to get bushes, Marjorie," my husband said as we finally trudged sadly down the hill. "Probably the best thing is just to plow it up and put in some grass." He dragged a log aside, began to rake. Then suddenly exclaimed. "Hey, look! They didn't *all* give up." And sure enough, here and there a bush still clung to the ravaged ground. Bowed, soiled, well-nigh rent apart, they not only held fast, a few were actually putting forth tiny new green leaves. And one a brave pink bloom!

"Oh, you brave little thing." I cried, kneeling to prop it up. And doing so, I smelled its fragrance. And a thrill of wonder and joy ran through me at the fierce will to survive that God puts into all living things, even the will to bloom and be beautiful again.

My husband and I looked at each other, smiling. We were both thinking the same thing. We'd start over, this whole garden would bloom again.

Lord, when life gets rough, when I too get bowed and beaten
by the storm, help me to remember those fearless roses.
—MAJORIE HOLMES, SEPTEMBER 2, 1982

One to Give

It is more blessed to give than to receive.

—ACTS 20:35

It was one of those gentle Georgia days on Granddaddy's farm, when the sun played behind the clouds, casting hazy orange shadows across the fields. I was picking cotton. I was only seven, and the burlap sack I pulled was lots bigger than I was. But I'd begged Granddaddy for the chance to pick, and he'd given in.

The cotton field stretched out ahead of me, shiny and green and freckled with white. There were lots of pickers in the field. They were paid by the pound, so their hands moved fast. They could skin a bush of its fluffy white balls before I could scratch my nose. Their sacks were growing fat. Mine was unmistakably thin. I wanted to quit. That's when an old Black woman idled up beside me, her hair tied in a faded red bandana.

"Mind if I pick with you?" she asked.

"No, ma'am," I said. "I don't guess so."

Her fingers worked like music down the row. But she did a curious thing. Every time she dropped a handful of cotton in her sack, she dropped one in mine as well. "One for you and one for me," she said.

My bag grew plump. I began to smile. But I was puzzled. So when we got to the plum tree shade at the fence, I said, "Why are you putting a handful in my sack each time you put one in yours?"

Her crinkled face smoothed out into a wide smile. "Child, don't you know your Bible? Don't you know the place where it says, 'Freely ye have received, freely give' (Matthew 10:8)? Remember this and don't forget: For every handful you take in life, that means you've got one to give."

And the child didn't forget. For sometimes when the taking in my life outweighs the giving, I remember, and I try to balance it up... *a handful of giving for every handful of taking.*

> *Lord, as I pull my little sack of need through this day,*
> *let me remember: one for You and one for me.*
> —SUE MONK KIDD, SEPTEMBER 21, 1982

1983

This year, Sally K. Ride became the first US woman in space, and Microsoft Word (which we're using to write this) was first released. The movie theaters and restaurants were deserted as we watched the final episode of *M*A*S*H**, the most watched episode in TV history. And in the first step in what would become a revolutionary transformation of everyday life, the FCC authorized Motorola to begin testing cellular phone service in Chicago.

When we were in the movie theater, we were watching *The Big Chill, Terms of Endearment, Fanny & Alexander* and *The Right Stuff,* while the books in our tote bags and briefcases were John Naisbitt's *Megatrends, In Search of Excellence* by Thomas J. Peters and Robert H. Waterman Jr., *Mistral's Daughter* by Judith Krantz, *The Little Drummer Girl* by John le Carré, *The Name of the Rose* by Umberto Eco, *Poland* by James Michener and, if we were looking for chills, *Pet Sematary* by Stephen King. Dancers were whirling to "Beat It" by Michael Jackson, "Flashdance—What a Feeling" by Irene Cara, "Every Breath You Take" by the Police and "Love Is a Battlefield" by Pat Benatar. For another year, a first-class stamp cost twenty cents.

Twenty-two writers joined us for *Daily Guideposts, 1983*. Series (monthly, weekly, and for Holy Week and Advent) had become established features of each year's edition. Two cherished writers, Phyllis Hobe and Drue Duke, made their first appearances, as did our popular journaling pages.

We've chosen three very distinguished names to represent *Daily Guideposts, 1983*. Arthur Gordon had a most *noteworthy* career. A native of Savannah, Georgia, graduate of Yale and a Rhodes Scholar, he was not only editor-in-chief and editorial director of *Guideposts*, he had also been editor of *Good Housekeeping* and *Cosmopolitan*, and the author of fourteen books, including the classic *A Touch of Wonder*. He graced us with his elegant devotionals in almost every edition of *Daily Guideposts* from 1979 until his death at age eighty-nine in 2002. Here we find him sitting on a little dock overlooking a creek and learning something profound from a family of raccoons.

Norman Vincent Peale was an American institution. Minister of New York City's Marble Collegiate Church for more than fifty years, Dr. Peale became "minister to millions" through his weekly Sunday radio broadcasts. His book *The Power of Positive Thinking*, a megabest seller since its publication in 1952, is still in print today. Along with his wife Ruth Stafford Peale, Dr. Peale founded Guideposts in 1945, and his devotionals appeared in *Daily Guideposts* from 1979 to 1994. An enthusiastic traveler, Dr. Peale found inspiration everywhere he went, as in this visit to a Danish cathedral.

Writer and journalist Elaine St. Johns wasn't afraid to speak her mind, a trait she shared with her mother, Adela Rogers

St. Johns, an intrepid reporter in the 1920s and 1930s and a noted Hollywood screenwriter. Elaine's *Prayer Can Change Your Life*, written with Dr. William R. Parker, has done just that for many. This devotional about her mother and her infantryman brother during World War II is a reminder to all of us to keep on praying.

Tough Love

Now no chastening for the present seemeth to be joyous,
but grievous: nevertheless afterward it yieldeth
the peaceable fruit of righteousness....
—HEBREWS 12:11

The other day, sitting quietly on our little dock that overlooks a tidal creek, I saw a mother raccoon lead her three babies out of the tall grass on the far side of the creek and onto a fallen tree that stretched out to deep water. She dove in gracefully and swam around, chirring at the little ones, coaxing them to join her. They just looked dismayed; obviously they had never tried to swim. This was to be their first lesson.

The mother climbed back up on the tree, took one baby in her mouth and swam across the creek with it. She did the same with the second. The third waited expectantly for his free ride, but nothing happened. The mother called to him from the far bank; she didn't go back to him. He grew increasingly agitated, crying piteously and dipping one timid paw into the tide. The mother's answering calls became fainter. She was leaving him—or so she seemed to want him to think.

Finally, with a desperate plunge, the baby threw himself into the creek and floundered frantically to shore, where I was sure that in a minute or two he would brag to his siblings about how brave he was.

An analogy? I think so. That raccoon mother chose the toughest of her babies for her little lesson in loving. She tested him because she knew he could respond. She seemed to abandon him, but she never did.

Need I go on...?

Dear Lord, when I think You have forgotten me,
let me remember that baby raccoon.
—ARTHUR GORDON, JANUARY 8, 1983

The Arms of the Savior

If any man hear my voice, and open the door, I will come in
to him, and will sup with him, and he with me.

—REVELATION 3:20

*W*henever I'm in Denmark, I make an effort to go to
Copenhagen's great Protestant cathedral, *Vor Frue Kirken*. Around its
walls are a series of colossal statues of the twelve apostles. They face
the central statue on the high altar, that of Jesus Christ.

There's an interesting story about the creation of that particular
work. Its sculptor, Bertel Thorvaldsen, in preparing his clay model,
had created a Jesus figure with arms raised high in a gesture of impe-
rious leadership. Pleased with his accomplishment, he left his studio
to let the soft clay harden overnight. When he returned in the morning, however, he was startled to find that Jesus' arms, the arms that
Thorvaldsen had so carefully fashioned into a stance of authority, had
drooped. They no longer commanded; no, they seemed to have fallen
into a gesture of pleading.

At first Thorvaldsen was bitterly disappointed. But they say something amazing happened to him as he stood gazing at the transformed

statue. He now saw before him the image of the *true* Jesus, the man of compassion. At that moment Bertel Thorvaldsen became a Christian. And eventually he was led to chisel on the base of the finished statue, "Come unto Me."

No, Jesus does not command *us to follow Him. He* invites *us.*
It is the most important, most beautiful, most rewarding
invitation you and I will ever receive.
Jesus, I accept.
—NORMAN VINCENT PEALE, JANUARY 16, 1983

At the Crossroads

Stand ye still, and see the salvation of the Lord with you...
fear not, nor be dismayed...
for the Lord will be with you.
—II CHRONICLES 20:17

*E*very night during World War II my mother went to her Bible in search of guidance for her sons in the service. She would read and then pray specifically for one of them. Around midnight on Thanksgiving Eve in 1944 she was reading the above Scripture and praying for my brother Mac, who was marching with General Patton's army across France.

The sergeant of a reconnaisance platoon, Mac was standing in the middle of a road, ready to lead his men through some woods to a cross-road beyond which an enemy strong point was suspected to be. A seasoned soldier, Mac knew it was against all rules to move down that road in plain sight, normal procedure called for fanning his men out so they could move through that cover of the woods in a shallow wedge. Yet for no apparent reason, after standing in thought for a moment, he walked them right down the middle of the road in a column.

They found that the crossroad was unoccupied and turned to walk back. There, on the reverse sides of the trees, they saw the signs, *Minen!*—posted to warn German soldiers approaching from that direction that the woods were mined. "Had we gone through them," Mac wrote in an exchange of letters, "we would have been blown apart. Keep praying for me, Mother. He is with us—and with you."

It is good to know that You hear those who are praying for me,
Father. Sometimes all I can do is stand still for
that moment and follow Your guidance.
—ELAINE ST. JOHNS, JANUARY 17, 1983

1984

This year had a sinister ring for those of us who had read George Orwell's novel *1984*. Orwell's bleak vision was put to good satiric use as the year began when Apple introduced its user-friendly Macintosh personal computer in an epic Super Bowl commercial. Later in the year, in retaliation for our boycott of the 1980 Moscow Olympic Games, the Soviet Union and its allies withdrew from the Summer Olympic Games in Los Angeles. In the wake of the storming of the Golden Temple in Amritsar, Indian Prime Minister Indira Gandhi was assassinated. And in November, President Reagan was reelected in a landslide with 59 percent of the vote.

Readers were snapping up such memoirs as Edward Koch's *Mayor* and Lee Iacocca's *Iacocca*, such novels as *The Aquitaine Progression* by Robert Ludlum, *Full Circle* by Danielle Steel, *"...and Ladies of the Club"* by Helen Hooven Santmeyer, *First Among Equals* by Jeffrey Archer, *The Fourth Protocol* by Frederick Forsyth and *The Talisman* by Stephen King. Hot tickets at the movies included *Amadeus, The Killing Fields, A Passage to India* and *The Pope of Greenwich Village*. Hit tunes included "What's Love Got to Do with It" by Tina Turner, "Can't Slow Down" by Lionel Richie, "Girls Just Want to Have Fun" by Cyndi Lauper, "Jump" by the Pointer Sisters, and "Dancing in the Dark" by Bruce Springsteen. We could still use those twenty-cent stamps to mail a first-class letter.

An even two dozen writers graced *Daily Guideposts, 1984.* For the first time we had a theme, "The Parables," which we learned to appreciate more deeply in Arthur Gordon and Fred Bauer's monthly series "Jesus the Master Storyteller." And each month *Guideposts* Editor-in-Chief Van Varner's "Guidepeople" took us behind the scenes at the magazine.

Patricia Houck Sprinkle and her minister-husband Bob lived in Atlanta, where she helped nurture the fledgling Evangelical Covenant Church of the Resurrection, worked to alleviate world hunger and raised two active boys. In the 1984 devotional included here, she writes about one of her spiritual heroes, who taught not so much in words as in gentle acts of kindness.

Whenever Arthur Gordon put pen to paper, words of love, hope, faith and kindness poured out. He followed the great psychiatrist Karl Menninger's description of his purpose in life: "to try to dilute the misery of the world." And he did so with the positive outlook he got from his mentor Norman Vincent Peale: "All things are possible with God"—as in this example of healing prayer.

Daily Guideposts readers practically grew up with Marion Bond West's family—the twins Jeremy and Jon and daughters Julie and Jennifer, many dogs and cats and, after her husband Jerry passed away, her second husband Gene. Marion's faith has gotten her through many difficulties, and here she gathers the whole family to look up to the heavens.

A Lesson in Preaching

My little children, let us not love in word, neither in tongue;
but in deed and in truth.

—I JOHN 3:18

*L*egend tells us that once a zealous young man went to St. Francis of Assisi and implored the saint to teach him how to preach.

"Gladly," said Francis. "Come with me."

All afternoon the young man followed Francis about, waiting eagerly for his lesson. They paused beneath a tree, and Francis stooped to return a young bird to its nest. They went on and stopped in a field crowded with reapers, and Francis bent his back to help the laborers load the hay onto a cart. From there they went to the town square, where Francis lifted a bucket of water from the well for an old woman and carried it home for her.

Each time they stopped, the young man was certain that a sermon would be forthcoming—but no words of great truth or wise discourse issued from the saint's mouth. Finally they went into the church—but Francis only knelt silently to pray.

At last, they returned to the place from whence they had started. "But when," the young man, by now thoroughly perplexed, asked the saint, "are you going to teach me how to preach?"

Francis smiled. "I just did."

Dear Lord, make my life a sermon—this day.
—PATRICIA HOUCK SPRINKLE, JULY 19, 1984

Strength in the Stillness

They shall run, and not be weary.

—ISAIAH 40:31

Fatigue—just plain physical tiredness—is a problem for many people. Did you know that there is a spiritual remedy for it?

One day, Roy Lawrence, an English minister interested in spiritual healing, went to visit an old lady in Cornwall named Carrie Oates. Carrie, spry as a cricket at the age of eighty-two, had been healed of glaucoma by the laying on of hands, and she herself possessed a remarkable gift of healing.

"My gift," she told Roy Lawrence, "is to draw people into the stillness of God's presence. The highest form of prayer is contained in the words 'Be still and know that I am God.'"

About fatigue, Carrie Oates had this to say: "When you're tired, sit down for a few minutes, close your eyes and think of the presence of God, because He is everywhere. Dwell on the words 'made in the image of God' and 'the life of God in every cell.' There is no weariness in God—and if you let His strength flow into you, there will be no weariness in you either!"

Can your mind tell your body how to behave? Of course it can, and if the harmony of God dwells in your mind, it dwells also in your body.

Lord, fill me with the healing presence of Your harmony today.
—ARTHUR GORDON, JULY 30, 1984

Looking Up

The heavens declare the glory of God.

—PSALM 19:1

What an enchanting way to spend a summer evening! When I was a child, my mother would spread out an old quilt on the side lawn just before dark. Then she and I and some of the neighborhood children would lie down on it and gaze up at the heavens. Sometimes for hours.

"There's Orion," someone always observed. "Look, a falling star!" someone else marveled. "I used to look up at the very same stars when I was a little girl," my mother often told us. And then we would mull over all the people in the past who observed the same celestial glory. "Even the Lord Jesus Himself, when He was on earth, saw the stars just as we see them now," the elderly woman from next door pointed out. We never tired of it—lying on the old quilt and looking up into the silent, starry night.

The other evening I walked out of our air-conditioned den, away from the television, and spread out an old quilt on the lawn.

"What are you doing?" one of our teenaged sons asked nervously as he rode up on his bike. He glanced around cautiously to see whether any of the neighbors might be watching. "I'm going to look at the heavens," I announced calmly. He sat down beside me and followed my gaze upward. Our other son soon joined us. And my husband, who understands all about looking at the stars, quietly came from the house and sat down on the quilt. And after that, lo and behold, our nineteen-year-old daughter and her boyfriend plopped down beside us.

"There's Orion," my daughter said.

"Did you used to do this when you were a little girl, Mama?" one of the boys asked.

Deep, deep satisfaction and a wondrous sense of worship filled my heart.

Thank You, Father, for being the same
yesterday, today and forever.
—MARION BOND WEST, AUGUST 18, 1984

1985

Epochal changes began this year when Mikhail Gorbachev became the Soviet leader and initiated a broad program of reform and liberalization. In one of the all-time corporate gaffes, Coca-Cola changed its formula and released New Coke to an overwhelmingly negative response. In an effort to reduce soaring deficits, the US Congress enacted a budget-balancing bill.

Readers had their noses in *The Sicilian* by Mario Puzo, *If Tomorrow Comes* by Sidney Sheldon, *Family Album* by Danielle Steel, *Hold the Dream* by Barbara Taylor Bradford, *Cider House Rules* by John Irving, *Lake Wobegone Days* by Garrison Keillor, and *Elvis and Me* by Priscilla Beaulieu Presley. At the movies, we watched *Kiss of the Spider Woman, Out of Africa, Prizzi's Honor* and *The Color Purple*, while we listened to "We Are the World" by USA for Africa, "Smooth Operator" by Sade, "Saving All My Love for You" by Whitney Houston, "Why

Not Me" by the Judds and "Unguarded" by Amy Grant. In February, the price of a first-class stamp went up to twenty-two cents.

Our twenty-six writers explored "Everyday Discipleship" in *Daily Guideposts, 1985*, led by Patricia Houck Sprinkle's series "The Everyday Disciple." Arthur Gordon started each month with some practical pointers to "New Beginnings," and Van Varner—a Kentucky native who became the quintessential New Yorker—invited us to "Meet Me in the City." Marilyn Morgan Helleberg helped us to see "Easter through the Eyes of Jesus and Mary," and Sue Monk Kidd invited us to spend a week with the Lord's Prayer. We traveled down the Mississippi with Fred Bauer, who showed us later in the year "Where to Find Christmas." What's now our Fellowship Corner appeared as the Family Album, with chatty bios and photos of our writers, among whom for the first time appeared *Guideposts* magazine newcomer (and now executive editor) Rick Hamlin.

One of our three representatives of 1985 is someone we've met before: Eleanor Sass. Ellie lived life exuberantly—traveling to Costa Rica to save endangered sea turtles, to Colorado for skiing, to England to present her grandfather's Bible to her British cousins. But as she shows us here, her favorite time was 9:45 on Monday mornings when the Guideposts staff gathered to pray for the needs of our readers.

During his years as *Guideposts* magazine's editor-in-chief, Van Varner kept its trademark first-person stories trim and to the point, and that's the way he wrote his devotionals. His love for and knowledge of his adopted city were boundless, and every year in May, you could find Van at a most remarkable birthday party.

A simple man with a big heart, Sam Justice of Yonkers, New York, spent his retirement years reading his Bible, helping his wife Ginny around the house, driving his elderly neighbors to church, playing golf and writing for *Daily Guideposts*. He and Ginny raised five children, all successful today, but as you'll see, there were some hard lessons in parenting he had to learn along the way.

Prayer Fellowship

They shall lay hands on the sick, and they shall recover.

—MARK 16:18

Every Monday morning at 9:45 at the Guideposts offices in Carmel and New York City, the staff gathers around tables to read hundreds of letters that have come to us from all over the nation. These letters tell of important needs—for finding jobs, help with marriage problems, guidance with teenagers, healing, bereavement—and the writers are all asking the Guideposts Prayer Fellowship to pray for these needs.

One day not long ago a few of us here in New York were discussing the enormous number of prayer requests and wondering how we might feel closer, more personal ties to our unseen letter writers. One editor said that, at the point when we have a general prayer for all of the needs, he places his hands on top of his pile of letters. "I like to think that the Spirit of God is working through my hands and touching all of those lives."

The next Monday morning I copied my editor friend. I prayed that at that very moment, the people whose letters were under my hands would feel, really feel, our prayers.

Another Monday, a few weeks later, I picked up a praise letter, one of those letters that say, "Thank you for praying for me." And then I read the words that have encouraged me to continue the practice of placing my hands on all of my letters: "I really *felt* your prayers."

Thank You, Lord, for giving us new ways
to pray one for another.
—ELEANOR SASS, JANUARY 28, 1985

The Party on the Promenade

And God said, Let us make man in our image....
—GENESIS 1:26

After work this afternoon I'm going to a party for a 102nd birthday. The party is not for a person; it's for a thing, a bridge, the Brooklyn Bridge.

I've been attending this annual event for many years, ever since my friend Joe Caldwell came to town from Milwaukee and took up residence in a house on an old street that ran under the Manhattan side of the bridge. Hague Street is no longer there, and neither is Joe nor his house (progress!), but during the time Joe lived there he acquired an affection for this beautiful steel span, an affection that infected his friends, too, me included.

Joe could step onto "his" bridge from a certain window in his apartment, and often he'd be out there, strolling in the sun or walking in the fresh-fallen snow, listening to the music of the wind in steel filigree.

Today a group of us will meet midbridge on the elevated, wood-planked promenade. We'll put on funny paper hats and join in a proud salute to the giant granite towers. We'll also startle a few pedestrians, some of whom will be amused enough to join us, and some of whom will return to join us next year just as other passersby have done in the past.

Perhaps this all sounds very silly, a bit mad. Two years ago, however, when the Brooklyn Bridge became a hundred years old, our entire city went wild. Millions lined the waterfront, hundreds of boats thronged the river, and the most fantastical display of fireworks I've ever seen dazzled the sky in brilliant birthday tribute.

And why not? When man uses the talents that God gives him, and with wisdom and daring and sweat turns them into something as serviceable and beautiful and lasting as this bridge, why not celebrate? This year too.

Oh, those wondrous gifts of creativity and imagination that
You have entrusted to man, Lord God.
Let me use mine for Your glory.
—VAN VARNER, MAY 24, 1985

Letting Go

For in him we live, and move, and have our being...
For we are also his offspring.
—ACTS 17:28

In years past I used to worry relentlessly about my children: their lifestyles, their late hours, their friends, their lack of church attendance. Even though I tried to trust them to God, I couldn't help but feel that He could use some good stout assistance from me.

But things fell apart. When my eldest son was having problems and I thought he could benefit from *my* wisdom and *my* counsel, he rejected my sage advice and went his own way, getting himself into scrape after scrape. Finally he got good and tired of me and took off for Florida.

That really upset me, and I told God about it. His answer was: *You love him and trust Me.* Well, God did much better with my son than I did. Sometime after he finished college and went to work, I paid him a visit. I was amazed to see that—without any help whatsoever from me—he had accomplished so much. He must have read my mind, because he looked me right in the eye and said, "Thanks, Dad, for giving me up, but not giving up on me."

When we would worry after our children, Lord,
remind us that You are Father of each.
—SAM JUSTICE, JULY 18, 1985

1986

Tragedies dominated the news in 1986: A major nuclear accident at the Soviet Union's Chernobyl power station alarmed the world, while in the US, the space shuttle *Challenger* exploded after its launch at Cape Canaveral, Florida, killing the seven astronauts aboard.

On our TV screens, a national audience was introduced to Oprah Winfrey, while Fox, the fourth TV network, was born and offered ten hours of primetime programming a week. At the movies, we watched *Platoon, Hannah and Her Sisters, The Color of Money,* and *The Mission.* When we took our eyes off the little and big screens, we read *Fatherhood* by Bill Cosby, Dr. Seuss's *Your Only Old Once, The Bourne Supremacy* by Robert Ludlum, *A Perfect Spy* by John le Carré, *I'll Take Manhattan* by Judith Krantz and *Last of the Breed* by Louis L'Amour. On the top of the charts were "Higher Love" by Steve Winwood, "Graceland" by Paul Simon, "That's What Friends Are For" by Dionne Warwick, Elton John, Gladys Knight and Stevie Wonder, "Back Where You Started" by Tina Turner and "Addicted to Love" by Robert Palmer. A first-class stamp still cost twenty-two cents.

The theme our twenty-eight writers addressed as we celebrated our tenth anniversary was "Fellowship," and joining our fellowship for the first time was Carol Kuykendall of Boulder, Colorado. Sue Monk Kidd shared some ways of "Practicing the Presence of God"; Marilyn Morgan Helleberg took us on a "Wilderness Journey" with children of Israel; we learned about "The Seven Pillars of Marriage" that had blessed Dr. and Mrs. Peale; Arthur Gordon guided us through his beloved Savannah; Jeff Japinga led us through Holy Week and Patricia Houck Sprinkle through Advent.

Marilyn Morgan Helleberg (now Marilyn Morgan King) is one of our most thoughtful, contemplative writers, ever listening for the still, small voice of the Spirit. Over the years she's shared her own most personal journeys through illness, bereavement, divorce and eventual remarriage. Here she shares a wise physician's advice we could all profit from.

Arthur Gordon came from a distinguished Georgia family, and here he writes about his aunt, Juliette Gordon Low, who founded the Girl Scouts of America.

Carol Kuykendall was the mother of three when she began writing for us; she's now the grandmother of eight! From the very first, Carol has had the gift of telling a story that keeps us reading and never fails to deliver a fruitful thought to take into the day, as in the story we include here from her debut year.

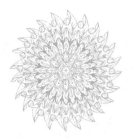

A Daily Dose of Prayer

Men ought always to pray....
—LUKE 18:1

I know a doctor who suggests to his patients and their families that they go home and pray after they have been treated. It's part of his prescription for them. One day last week he told me that two different people objected to that suggestion. One, a father whose child had strep throat, said, "Why pray? That penicillin shot will cure him." The other was the husband of a terminally ill cancer patient, who said, "What good could prayer do at this point?"

"It never occurred to these people," said my doctor-friend, "that prayer could be something more than begging God for favors, that it could be a way of tapping into undreamed-of potentials within themselves, a chance to bind themselves to something greater than their bodies or individual egos, to glimpse the wonder and mystery and hope that is God. No matter how many 'miracle drugs' there are, no matter how hopeless an illness is, there will always be a need for the belief, the wonder, the faith, that expresses itself in prayer."

Great Physician, I will daily take my dosage of prayer,
for healing of spirit as well as body.
—MARILYN MORGAN HELLEBERG, APRIL 29, 1986

Aunt Daisy's Girls

Remember now thy Creator in the days of thy youth. . . .
—ECCLESIASTES 12:1

*T*here's a lovely old house downtown where two stone lions guard the doorway, just the right size for a small boy to sit upon and imagine he is monarch of his own private kingdom. The house once belonged to my aunt Juliette Gordon Low, who was founder of the Girl Scouts of America. And I was the little boy with the big imagination. The lions were British lions because my aunt's father-in-law, who built the house around 1840, was an English merchant. The lions are still there but, now that the Colonial Dames own the house, nobody rides them anymore.

Aunt Daisy, as we called her, died when I was fifteen, but I remember her vividly—warm, spirited, very deaf, but full of the joy of living. Aunt Daisy had no children of her own, but she had millions of adopted ones: Girl Scouts. They were always around in their (then) khaki-colored uniforms, and Aunt Daisy was always busy with them: feeding them, teaching them, showing the girls ways to be their best.

She was an animal lover too. She had a mockingbird that would sit on her shoulder and nibble at her pen as she wrote letters. And a huge, somewhat malevolent parrot called Polly Poons. And countless dogs. All living things were loved and cared for by Aunt Daisy's generosity and goodness.

I recall Aunt Daisy once gave me a strong-willed pony named Buster Brown. When Buster Brown didn't get his way, he would rear up and fall on his back. I learned to be very good at jumping off in a hurry. When I complained to Aunt Daisy about this, she explained solemnly that ponies and horses see everything eight times its normal size, and so they're easily frightened. This struck me as a reasonable explanation, and I forgave Buster Brown everything...which was what she wanted me to do, of course.

At night, when I used to conclude my small-boy prayers with a list of people I wanted God to bless, Aunt Daisy was always on my list. Her love and zest for life lives on in my small-boy's heart, and her legacy to all American girls has touched countless generations, from town to town, city to city, across our land.

Lord, let my life be an inspiration to others.
—ARTHUR GORDON, AUGUST 24, 1986

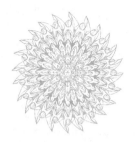

Baby Steps

And let us run with patience the race that is set before us.
—HEBREWS 12:1

Sometime early in my thirty-ninth year, I decided to run a half-marathon. I guess I needed a physical challenge, and a thirteen-mile race seemed a respectable goal for an inconsistent, fair-weather jogger like me. So I picked a mid-October race and began to train. On nice days, at least. And I prayed, "Lord, please give me the perseverance to reach this goal."

The day of the race dawned, sleet-gray and spitting frost. "That's it," I announced. "I'm staying home."

But somehow I couldn't.

So off I went to the starting line, all bundled up and reluctant. The gun went off and I moved out with the throng. The wind blew stinging ice crystals in my face. The miles began to pass by. Slowly. Four . . . then five. I wanted to quit.

But again I couldn't.

"Just take little baby steps," a voice inside commanded. "Keep moving forward toward the goal."

Somehow I kept going. One jogging step at a time. At Mile 10, my legs felt like jelly. My lungs screamed with every gulp of frigid air. I wanted to quit.

But I couldn't.

"Baby steps," said the voice. "Don't stop." Mile 11...12...only one more to go. I saw the finish line in the distance. With a burst of energy I crossed it, numb with cold but exhilarated, and thankful that the voice inside me hadn't let me quit.

> *Lord, even when I'm tired and discouraged, help me persevere toward my goal, albeit one baby step at a time.*
> —CAROL KUYKENDALL, OCTOBER 2, 1986

1987

In Washington, DC, Oliver North Jr. told a congressional inquiry that higher officials had approved his secret Iran-Contra operations; President Ronald Reagan admitted that Iran arms-Contra policy went astray and accepted responsibility. The US Supreme Court ruled that Rotary Clubs must admit women.

On the fiction best-seller lists were two by Stephen King, *The Eyes of the Dragon* and *Misery*, *Windmills of the Gods* by Sidney Sheldon, *Fine Things* by Danielle Steel, *The Haunted Mesa* by Louis L'Amour, and *Presumed Innocent* by Scott Turow. On the nonfiction lists were John Feinstein's *A Season on the Brink*, *The Closing of the American Mind* by Allen Bloom, and Whitley Streiber's *Communion*. We lined up at the theater to see *Moonstruck*, *Wall Street*, *The Last Emperor* and *Fatal Attraction*, and at music stores to buy "Somewhere Out There" by Linda Ronstadt and James Ingram, "I Wanna Dance with Somebody" by Whitney Houston, "Bring on the Night" by Sting, and "(I've Had) the Time of My Life" by Jennifer Warnes and Bill Medley. Twenty-two cents still bought a first-class stamp.

Forty writers prepared the bill of fare for *Daily Guideposts, 1987,* and a rich one it was. Our theme was "God's Everlasting Love," and Phyllis Hobe's monthly "Lessons in Love" traced it through the year. Eleanor Sass gave us monthly "Bible Echoes," while Sue Monk Kidd traversed Holy Week and Advent. There were special series by Van Varner, John and Elizabeth Sherrill, and Elaine St. Johns; Norman Vincent Peale added praises of the four seasons. And new to the family were Patricia Lorenz and Linda Ching Sledge.

Oscar Greene has been a quiet, beloved presence in *Daily Guideposts* since 1981. A retired technical writer, Oscar's devotionals glow with his love for his wife Ruby, his church family and his neighbors in West Medford, Massachusetts, and honestly relate his struggles as an African American seeking to find his way in a still-segregated America. And he shares his love for sports, as in this 1987 devotional about his grandson Shawn and a basketball hero.

Our second 1987 devotional comes from readers' favorite Sue Monk Kidd, who tells us a story of a frisky puppy, an untimely death and a thoughtful—and providential—gift of consolation.

The author of more than 1,500 articles and thirty books, many cowritten with her husband John, including such classics as *The Hiding Place, The Cross and the Switchblade,* and *God's Smuggler,* Elizabeth (Tib) Sherrill has been a writer and editor for *Guideposts* for more than fifty years, and has helped nurture generations of inspirational writers as a teacher at the Guideposts Writers Workshop. Blessed with a remarkable eye for the spiritual heart of the situations and people she's met in her travels all over the world, she writes devotionals filled with grace and a simple eloquence, as in this 1987 account of a moving encounter with one of America's most famous theologians.

Small Boy, Big Man

Before honour is humility.
—PROVERBS 15:33

When our grandson Shawn was ten, he enrolled in a week-long basketball camp in New Hampshire. There two hundred youngsters practiced basketball from morning to evening. All of them looked forward to the highlight of the week, when a basketball celebrity would visit the camp.

M. L. Carr from the champion Boston Celtics was scheduled to appear this particular week, and parents—and grandparents—were invited to attend. Shawn was almost wild with excitement. "Do you think he'll give me his autograph, Grampa?" he asked.

I didn't know what the camp's policy toward autograph-seekers was, so I got out of it gracefully. "Just don't make a pest of yourself," I advised.

The day came, and the famous visitor was to play a youngster one-on-one, with the other campers observing. (One-on-one means two people play until one of them scores ten baskets.) Mr. Carr looked over the group and chose our Shawn. Shawn was so happy he was ready to explode.

But the best was yet to come. When the matchup ended, the towering Mr. Carr leaned over and shook Shawn's hand. "Shawn, you're a great player," he said. "May I have your autograph?" An elated Shawn wrote his name on Mr. Carr's sneaker.

Now we all know that Mr. Carr is a "big man" in the world's eyes. But by this act of grace, in deferring to the pride of a small boy, he made himself a big man in the eyes of the Lord.

Heavenly Father; help me to learn humility, so that I may place the achievements of others ahead of my own.
—OSCAR GREENE, JUNE 4, 1987

Murph

And God shall wipe away all tears from their eyes.

—REVELATION 7:17

My husband brought him home one day in a cardboard box: a baby beagle with wistful brown eyes and Dumbo ears. I lifted him out and held him against my shoulder. From that moment, the two of us became special friends.

We often sat on the grass beside the rose vine in the backyard, Murph napping while I read. Once he gnawed a rose and pricked his nose on a thorn. He looked at me so bewildered.

The children fixed a basket, so Murph could ride along when I picked them up from school. But he never stayed in it. He always put his paws up to the window, wagging his tail at the scenery. But one day Murph lay in his basket and didn't get up. By evening he was very sick.

The next morning I carried him to the vet. "Better leave him with me," the vet said. Murph looked at me the way he did that day he was pricked by the thorn. The next day he died.

After the vet called, I walked outside to the rose vine, looking, I suppose, for some bit of comfort. But all the roses were dead. I could not find a single one that wasn't brown and wilted. It left me utterly sad, and when I shuffled back inside, I could hardly see through my tears.

It was noon when I heard a sound at my door. When I answered it, I saw, there on the steps, a jar of fresh red roses. Beautiful *living* roses. As I gazed at them, an inexplicable comfort began to pour through me...a vivid sense of life's beauty and joy. I looked along the street, mystified.

Later that day my friend Betty called. "I was in the garden, praying," she told me, "when God seemed to insist that I bring you some roses."

As I hung, up, I was sure. No matter what thorny places we walk, God never leaves us in our pain. He sends His comfort one way or another.

Dear God, Thank You for the comfort You bring at life's hurts,
for the delight You bring at life's beauty.
—SUE MONK KIDD, JULY 6, 1987

The Power of Silence

Blessed be God, even the Father of our Lord Jesus Christ,
the Father of mercies, and the God of all comfort;
Who comforteth us in all our tribulation....

—II CORINTHIANS 1:3–4

Heavy snow was falling that night as we drove toward New York City. John's father had died of a heart attack an hour earlier. *What can we possibly say to Mother at such a time?* we wondered in the midst of our own shock.

She met us at the door to their apartment at Union Theological Seminary, where Dad taught. After dinner that evening, she told us, they'd gone for a walk in the snow. Two hours later, Dad complained of pain in his chest. The doctor had arrived too late.

We groped for words of comfort, but none came. At last, feeling that we'd failed her, we went to bed, there in the apartment.

The following morning the doorbell rang at seven. Standing in the hallway was Reinhold Niebuhr. A fellow professor at Union, this renowned theologian was well-versed in the mysteries of life and death. He would be able to put into words all that we could not.

I led Dr. Niebuhr into the living room and went to call John and his mother. We all took chairs while I waited eagerly to hear the words of Christian insight Dr. Niebuhr would pronounce. A minute passed. Two minutes, while my expectation mounted. At last, with crooked arthritic fingers, he reached for Mother's hand.

"Well, Helen," he said—the very first words he had uttered.

Silence fell again. Five minutes...ten full minutes had elapsed, and still this gifted preacher had not shared his words of wisdom.

After fifteen minutes, the stillness of the room began to seep inside me until a wordless communion seemed to enfold us all. When the clock chimed the half hour, Dr. Niebuhr stood up and let himself out.

And still John and Mother and I sat silent. Not until the undertakers arrived just before eight did any of us speak, and then only to deal with the logistics of death. Later John and I would find the words of love and honoring that need to be spoken in their time.

For now, though, it was enough that we were there.

We had learned the power of silence from one of the great speakers of our century. Niebuhr had not come with words, no matter how lofty. He had brought instead the best, the costliest thing one person can give to another. He had brought himself.

Thank You, Lord, that You are Emmanuel...God with us.
—ELIZABETH SHERRILL, AUGUST 23, 1987

1988

In 1988, Benazir Bhutto, the first Islamic woman prime minister, was chosen to lead Pakistan while George H. W. Bush won the US presidential election as Republicans swept forty states. In December, a terrorist bomb destroyed a Pan-Am 747 over Lockerbie, Scotland, killing all 259 aboard.

Rainman, Mississippi Burning, A Fish Called Wanda and *Bull Durham* were playing in theaters; "Don't Worry Be Happy" by Bobby McFerrin, "Faith" by George Michael, "Fast Car" by Tracy Chapman, "Brasil" by the Manhattan Transfer and "Simply Irresistible" by Robert Palmer were playing on our radios; *Moonwalk* by Michael Jackson, physicist Stephen Hawking's *A Brief History of Time, The Bonfire of the Vanities* by Tom Wolfe, *The Icarus Agenda* by Robert Ludlum, *Alaska* by James Michener, *The Cardinal and the Kremlin* by Tom Clancy, and *The Queen of the Damned* by Anne Rice were in the bookstores. In April, first-class postage went up to twenty-five cents.

"The Family" was the theme our *Daily Guideposts* family of forty-nine writers addressed in 1988, with special contributions by Carol Kuykendall ("Tandem Power") and Floyd and Harriett Thatcher ("Family Time"). Among the family's new members were soon-to-be-regulars Carol Knapp, who brought the Alaska wilderness to *Daily Guideposts*, college teacher Daniel Schantz and Indiana's Mary Lou Carney.

Van Varner was a passionate New Yorker, but he also had a great love of horses, especially the thoroughbreds whose grace and speed made Derby Day the highlight of the year in his native Kentucky. One horse in particular had captured his imagination as a boy, and prompted the pilgrimage he described in his 1988 devotional.

This year brought a fresh new voice to *Daily Guideposts*: a Guideposts Writers Workshop winner who had recently moved to a home in the woods in Big Lake, Alaska. Carol Knapp showed us the hand of God in the wilderness through fresh eyes awake to the glories of creation: the mountains surrounding Katchemak Bay, the clear waters of Big Lake, moose idling by a remote chalet, and here, the most majestic mountain of them all.

Born in Hawaii, Linda Ching Sledge has made her mark as a novelist and as a professor of literature and writing. She and her husband Gary, a longtime *Reader's Digest* editor who has also written for *Daily Guideposts*, raised two sons in suburban Pleasantville, New York. In her 1988 devotional, Linda tells us how she and Gary fared at a summer dance class.

Big Red

And God saw every thing that he had made, and,
behold, it was very good.

—GENESIS 1:31

When I was a skinny eighteen-year-old fresh in the service during World War II, I made an impetuous trip to see a boyhood hero of mine. With a precious pass in my uniform pocket, I thumbed my way on empty Georgia roads, sat up all night on an unheated Southern Railway coach, but finally pulled into Lexington, Kentucky. At the USO, a motherly-looking volunteer was just opening up. "Please, ma'am," I said, "can you tell me how I can find Man O'War?"

Would you believe that nice woman couldn't believe I'd made the long trip just to see him? Only the greatest thoroughbred that ever lived, that's all! He was old, twenty-seven, and I had to see him before either he or I died. That's the way we were in wartime.

Well, there were all kinds of phone calls with talk about gas coupons, but soon I was being driven out to Faraway Farm where an old black man, Will Harbut, was actually waiting for me. Will was Man O'War's friend and groom—they were never apart. In a large green-painted shed, we crossed to a stall where Will rolled back the door.

"Okay, soldier boy, here he is, 'Big Red,' de mostest hoss."

I stared, mouth open.

Will talked at length about "Red's" speed, his stamina, his courage. I stared at the hero I'd come so far to see. And heroic he was, a massive animal with a coat of polished copper, a head held high, eyes looking beyond me with an imperial gaze. And ancient he was (a human would have been in his nineties) but the fire was still there.

"Come on," Will said, "it's okay," and I reached out and placed my hand on the head of Man O'War.

It's a good thing to have heroes. Seeing that great thoroughbred gave my life romance, ardor. It even deepened my faith in the Almighty, for no one could look at Man O'War without knowing that only God could create an animal so powerful, and yet so noble.

Lord, teach us to know Your masterpieces,
and feel reverence.
—VAN VARNER, JANUARY 7, 1988

The Everlasting Rock

Trust in the Lord for ever, for the
Lord God is an everlasting rock.
—ISAIAH 26:4 (RSV)

We were loading the airplane for the flight home after spending an idyllic weekend with friends at their remote chalet in the Alaskan bush. I kept glancing back at the cabin set among the trees, staunchly shouldering five feet of snow. *A person could hide away from life's problems in a place like that,* I thought. Since our arrival two days earlier I hadn't worried once about our struggling business. I had even managed to forget the bare pantry shelves at home. Now I was flying back to grim reality. No wonder I was reluctant to leave.

Skis bounced along the makeshift runway, lifting us effortlessly into blue sky. Below us, frozen rivers glistened in the sun. Forests of dark spruce spread across boundless stretches of windblown snow. Occasionally the blurred shape of a moose emerged from the trees. A miniature sled-dog team steadily wove a trail through a winding mountain pass.

Looming in the distance, overseeing all this vast domain, towered Mt. McKinley, or Denali, the "Great One." It made me think of God and His greatness. Names like Rock...Shield...Fortress...Stronghold marched through my mind. My worries seemed to shrink beneath the gaze of the immense mountain with the broad sweep of wilderness sprawling at its feet.

I thought how insurmountable my problems appear to me, on the ground, and how temporary they must look to God, Who sees my life from eternity's heights. Like Denali, God is a Rock rising high above His vast creation...but unlike Denali, our Great One is alive and endures evermore!

You are the solid Rock Who overshadows and outlasts
life's every rocky twist.
—CAROL KNAPP, MARCH 14, 1988

Two Left Feet

Let them praise his name with dancing....

—PSALM 149:3 (RSV)

I love to dance. But my husband Gary has two left feet and as much grace as a potato.

It's the one thing—the only thing—in our twenty-year marriage that I regret. He can't dance! So when a group of couples from church invited us to take a dance class at the local high school, I jumped. It took days of pleading to get Gary to go. But he did, knowing how much it meant to me. Visions began to rise in my head: Gary and I twirling, dipping, gracefully stepping around the dance floor, a 1980s "Ginger and Fred."

My aching feet soon told me we had made a big mistake. No matter what step we learned, Gary couldn't do it. Not the waltz. Not the lindy. Not the tango. And definitely not the samba! Our teacher was stumped. "I've never seen anything like it!" he told Gary, who had managed to step on the foot of the woman—and the man—behind us.

For eight weeks, Gary and I struggled on, while the other couples danced rings around us. The last night, we were to learn the hustle.

"I saved the hardest for last," our teacher warned, eyeing Gary sadly. Gary insisted that we try. He hadn't given up on himself, even though everyone else had.

The last class began like the others, with our friends gliding easily into the review steps, and Gary and I clomping along in our corner, two beats behind everybody else. Then the teacher lined us up in rows and taught us the hustle. After a few laborious tries, everyone groaned! No one could manage the complicated steps. No one, that is. . .

Except Gary! Everyone stood amazed as he stepped alone again and again to the tricky rhythms. With a brilliant grin, he reached for my hand, and pulled me expertly into a turn, and suddenly we were dancing! Really dancing! Just like Ginger and Fred!

*Lord, sometimes I cannot move to the rhythms of the rest of
the world. Give me the grace and confidence
to master the rhythm You have set aside for me alone.*
—LINDA CHING SLEDGE, AUGUST 19, 1988

1989

The most visible symbol of the division of Europe between East and West, the Berlin Wall, fell in 1989 as the Soviet empire continued to unravel. General Colin Powell became the first African American chairman of Joint Chiefs of Staff. In Beijing, thousands died as the democracy movement was crushed in Tiananmen Square. And comedienne Lucille Ball, one of the iconic figures of postwar America, died at age seventy-seven.

Moviegoers in 1989 viewed *Glory, Born on the Fourth of July, My Left Foot, Sex, Lies, and Videotape,* and *Field of Dreams*; readers devoured *Midnight* by Dean R. Koontz, *The Satanic Verses* by Salman Rushdie, *While My Pretty One Sleeps* by Mary Higgins Clark, *The Russia House* by John le Carré, *Polar Star* by Martin Cruz Smith, David Halberstam's *The Summer of '49*, and *My Turn* by Nancy Reagan; listeners heard "Wind Beneath My Wings" by Bette Midler, "Nick of Time" by Bonnie Raitt, "How Am I Supposed to Live without You" by Michael Bolton, and "Don't Know Much" by Linda Ronstadt and Aaron Neville. It still cost twenty-five cents to buy a first-class stamp.

As in 1988, forty-nine writers contributed to *Daily Guideposts,* *1989*'s exploration of "A Closer Walk with God." Walking with us for the first time were Eric Fellman and Linda Neukrug. We had monthly series by Mary Lou Carney ("Becoming as a Child Again") and Sue Monk Kidd ("Learning to Wait on God"); Phyllis Hobe showed us what Jesus might do in some contemporary situations; Linda Ching Sledge took us to islands she had visited or lived on; Fred Bauer shed light on Jesus' words by thinking about "What Jesus Didn't Say"; Elizabeth Sherrill brought us to "Easter: Road Map for Living"; and Marilyn Moore Jensen took us "On the Walk to Bethlehem." And as a "Back-to-School Bonus," four fifth-graders gave us stories in September.

Don Bell, a cowboy through and through, came to us in 1987. He loved horses, the open range and rodeos, and he wrote about his adventures in many magazines, including *Guideposts*. At age seventy-eight, he published a book of poems, *Reflections of a Cowboy*. Don battled cancer and died in April 2005 at age ninety-three. As he told his readers, "I'll ride this storm until it takes me home."

In his career as a journalist and author or coauthor of biographies and memoirs, Fred Bauer met many of the great men and women of faith of the second half of the twentieth century, including Billy Graham, gospel singer George Beverly Shea, artist Joni Eareckson Tada, poet Helen Steiner Rice, and many others. Here he recalls a conversation with best-selling author and Guideposts colleague Catherine Marshall.

Although the beauty of the wilderness always seems to bring out something special in Carol Knapp, she can write just as movingly about other, less serene aspects of life, as in her 1989 devotional about a dying man and God's special Christmas Eve gift.

Eyes on the Sparrow...
and on a Steer

How great are his signs! and how mighty are his wonders!
—DANIEL 4:3

I've heard it said that God keeps His eye on the sparrow. I think He keeps it on all His creatures, sometimes in ways that are hard to understand.

Back in 1958, I was a range cowboy looking after a bunch of steers for a man by the name of Smoky Grabbert, who ranched in Emblem, Wyoming. I had moved three hundred head of Angus steers to Dry Creek for summer pasture. Later I would have to move them to the mountains, so one day I rode through the Pitchfork Ranch Range country getting acquainted with the land so I would know the shortest way.

As I rode alone through this big country, I noticed a two-year-old Hereford steer stuck in a quicksand hole. Pitchfork Range had many of these dangerous holes; we called them soapholes. Today these holes are fenced, but back then they were open. This steer had stopped struggling, so I roped his head and tried to pull him out, but my horse was not stout enough to move this eight-hundred-pound critter.

I rode back to camp to get a four-wheel-drive pickup, chains, shovel and a hoist. I drove back at breakneck speed, as I knew the steer would soon sink and die. Lo and behold, as I approached, I saw the steer standing on dry land some distance from the soaphole. Perfectly safe!

To this day I don't know how that steer got out. I asked every Pitchfork cowboy, and no one had even been in that area. It made me realize that I wasn't the only one looking over that steer. Someone with much more power than I had taken care of that animal. His eye was on the sparrow, and it was on that steer too.

Father, keep reminding me when I forget and grow anxious or
fearful that Your eyes are on me, and I am in Your care,
no matter what comes.
—DON BELL, JANUARY 30, 1989

A Coincidence?

The earth is the Lord's, and everything in it, the world,
and all who live in it.
—PSALM 24:I (NIV)

*I*n the course of a lifetime we hear and read millions of words, yet only a few of them take up lodging in our hearts and minds. I was reminded of this the other day when a young woman, a very dedicated Christian, told me about some unexplainable occurrences in her life that figured in an important career decision. "It was a coincidence," she told me.

I asked her if she had ever thought about the meaning of coincidence—the convergence of two separate events. Then I told her about a conversation I had had with Catherine Marshall over afternoon tea many years ago. I was relating to her some strange twists and turns that had taken place in my life. "It is a coincidence that I am here," I said.

"A coincidence?" she pondered, circling the rim of her teacup, which tinkled like a fragile bell. "I doubt it. Always consider that God may be one of the partners of coincidence."

I've never forgotten what she told me. And whenever I hear some-one use the word *coincidence,* I want to share Catherine's spiritual in-sight. Like the teacup's tiny ring, the truth she spoke has continued to echo down through the years.

Give us ears, dear Lord, that recognize Your voice,
And trusting hearts that in Your will rejoice.
—FRED BAUER, SEPTEMBER 24, 1989

A Gift at Christmas

Rejoice with those who rejoice, weep with those who weep.
—ROMANS 12:15 (RSV)

The man in intensive care is dying. Overhead, erratic lines on a screen record the beat of his failing heart. The nurses' quick tread along the corridor mingles with the beep-beeping of the heart monitor. Not traditional Christmas Eve accompaniment, but then this is no ordinary Christmas Eve. The dying man is my father.

Sitting at his bedside, it seems incomprehensible that elsewhere people are eating and laughing and kissing under the mistletoe while my dad struggles to stay alive. At home, a husband and four young children are expecting my return to help them "celebrate."

I take my leave quietly at midnight, pausing an extra minute to memorize the unconscious face and to give a kiss minus the mistletoe.

On Christmas morning some joyous news. Dad rallied in the night, his condition had stabilized. When I walked into his room Christmas afternoon, he fluttered his eyes and managed a feeble "Hi, Carol." No tangible gift I have received before or since has even come close to the value of that weak hello. We were so thankful for the extra time with him we'd been granted, for he died five months later.

This year as you plan your holiday shopping, remember that you are the best gift you can give your family. And won't you join with me in praying for God's comfort to dwell with those who have loved ones who are infirm or in the hospital or who are facing Christmas without someone precious.

Heavenly Father, help us to pause amid our holiday merriment and give the gift of prayer for those whose Christmas isn't all rejoicing.
—CAROL KNAPP, DECEMBER 21, 1989

1990

As the Cold War waned, 1990 saw East Germany and West Germany reunited as a single country, and the first McDonald's opened in Moscow. In South Africa, freedom fighter Nelson Mandela was released from prison after twenty-seven years.

On our TV screens, *Seinfeld*, a very different and immensely popular sitcom premiered. We read George Will's *Men at Work*, *Trump: Surviving at the Top* by Donald Trump and Charles Leerhsen, *Devices and Desires* by P. D. James, *Oh, the Places You'll Go* by Dr. Seuss, *September* by Rosamunde Pilcher, *The Stand* by Stephen King, *The Burden of Proof* by Scott Turow and *The Plains of Passage* by Jean M. Auel. Our movie screens showed *Dances with Wolves*, *GoodFellas*, *Henry and June*, and *Reversal of Fortune*. Our CD players featured "Another Day in Paradise" by Phil Collins, "From a Distance" by Bette Midler, "Vision of Love" by Mariah Carey, "Oh, Pretty Woman" by Roy Orbison, "Twin Peaks Theme" by Angelo Badalamenti, "Bad Love" by Eric Clapton. We still paid twenty-five cents for a first-class stamp.

Our 1990 theme was "Windows," keynoted by Eleanor Sass's "Through an Open Window" and Marilyn Morgan Helleberg's "Windows into Wonder." Carol Kuykendall's "His Final Gestures" took us through Holy Week; Elizabeth Sherrill prepared us for Pentecost in "The Coming of the Spirit; and Terry Helwig encouraged us to "Journey to Inner Bethlehem." It was a year of journeys: We embarked on "A Family Adventure" with Eric Fellman and shared "Our Travels Together" with Ruth Stafford Peale. And we welcomed Arizonan Gina Bridgeman to our family circle.

We took a look behind the scenes this year, with devotionals by Terri Castillo and Stephanie Castillo Samoy (no relation). Terri, a longtime editor in Guideposts' book division, came to New York City from Kauai, Hawaii, and worked on *Daily Guideposts* from its beginning until 1995, by which time she had become its editor. Between her work and her studies, it was eight years before she returned home, and in this devotional, she wonders if she'll feel like a stranger.

Editor Stephanie Castillo Samoy has been a mainstay at Guideposts Books for more than twenty years. Originally from Tucson, Arizona, Stephanie, a multisport whiz, is the player-manager of the Guideposts softball team. Although she's a fierce competitor, Stephanie shows us here that she also knows there's more to a race than winning.

Over the years, *Daily Guideposts* has welcomed contributors from all walks of life—journalists, doctors, poets, engineers, students, ministers, retirees, stay-at-home moms and even a cowboy. John Coen of Wellsville, Kansas, was our resident farmer. He taught us about running an eighty-cow dairy farm and how sometimes the calf you love best is the one you have to give away.

Home Again

Be...children of light.
—JOHN 12:36

I hadn't been home to Hawaii in more than eight years. I was living and working in New York City, far away from my mother, six sisters and their children, some of whom I'd never met or were just tiny infants when I left. I was reluctant to return home. Would I be a strange outsider from the mainland, more like a tourist than a beloved *kamaaiina* (old-timer)?

My anxiety rose as the small inter-island jet touched down onto the newly built runway. A fancy, concrete structure greeted me, instead of the old, run-down wooden shack that was once the island's only commuter airport. *This homey little island has changed,* I thought uneasily to myself. I followed the signs through unfamiliar corridors to the baggage claim area and waited alone in silence until my luggage arrived. This did not feel like a welcome home at all.

Then a honk from the road, the patter of bare feet, and suddenly tiny arms wrapped around me, squeezing so hard I almost fell over. Small round faces with shiny black eyes and smiling mouths shouted in unison, "Auntie Tes! Auntie Tes!" They jumped up and down, garlanding my neck with sweet-smelling *leis*, strung by their tiny hands the night before. "We knew it was you! We've seen your pictures!" one of them·cried.

"Yeah," his sister agreed, "you're so pretty!" They grabbed for my attention: Two of the girls wanted me to admire their cartwheels, my youngest niece yelled a cheerleader's cheer, two nephews demonstrated a karate sequence, and another showed me his fancy football moves.

As I embraced my island family, the feeling of strangeness disappeared. I hadn't really been gone. Letters, phone calls, exchanged photographs had linked us to one another over the years. The children showed me how to make strangers feel welcomed: just bombard them with love.

I walked to the car, all my fears and hesitancies gone. "Now, Rico, I want to see one of your football games. And, girls, I want to attend your soccer meet. And the secret swimming hole, you'll take me there, won't you?..."

> *Father, let me be like a child in this world of strangers, and*
> *share my gifts of enthusiasm, excitement and*
> *encouragement with those around me.*
> —TERRI CASTILLO, MAY 18, 1990

A Run for the Fun of It

*Know ye not that they which run in a race run all, but one
receiveth the prize? So run, that ye may obtain.*
—I CORINTHIANS 9:24

*O*ur strategy is to start slow, go slow and finish slow," my friend
Nancy said to me with a laugh before the five-mile race in New York's
Central Park. This was the first race we'd ever entered, along with
eight hundred other runners from around the country.

At the starting line, I prayed that we'd at least finish the race and
possibly place. What was supposed to be a "fun run" had turned into
serious business for me. I wanted to leave my competitors in the dust.

The gun went off, and so did we. We were in the back of the pack,
but then I remembered Nancy's words about starting slow, going slow
and finishing slow. *Was she serious? Did she truly mean just to have a good
time?* I got my answer right from the start when she began to tell jokes
and stories as we ran side by side, and had me laughing uncontrollably.
Even those racers who were walking started to pass us.

By the first-mile marker, I knew my goal of placing was shattered,
and by the second-mile marker, Nancy had me stop for drinks of water

and to tighten shoelaces. Soon the finish line was in sight, and we decided to run our hardest.

Nancy beat me by a fraction of a second, but my disappointment was minimal. That was because she'd made me achieve our original goal of enjoying ourselves. Plus, God did answer my prayers; we placed 651st and 652nd.

> *God, when I run for the finish line, I pray that I'll do so with*
> *a strong faith, a kind heart and a jolly soul. What*
> *a winning combination that will be!*
> —STEPHANIE CASTILLO SAMOY, JUNE 23, 1990

Patsy's Calf

Even as the Son of man came . . . to give
his life a ransom for many.
—MATTHEW 20:28

As I care for my eighty Holsteins, I often remember my first calf. We didn't have a dairy, but even as a nine-year-old, I wanted to be a dairyman one day. So my dad and I headed over to our neighbor Jack's dairy farm. Jack took us into the calf barn where, back in the corner, were three Holstein heifers, each around three days old.

Jack said, "Now, Johnny, you can pick a calf and raise it as your own. But you have to give me back the first heifer calf she has." I had fallen in love with one calf in particular, and before we even had her loaded in the truck, I named her Patsy.

I bottle-fed Patsy, kept her stall clean and taught her to lead. I kept track of her feed records and veterinary expenses for my 4-H notebook. I couldn't have been prouder when I took Patsy to the county fair and showed her to all my friends.

As Patsy grew, I grew—both physically and in learning responsibility. Before I knew it, Patsy birthed a newborn baby heifer. I kept telling myself I wasn't going to become attached to her calf, but when I saw that new baby standing there, it was just as when I first laid eyes on Patsy. When the calf was four days old, we took it back to Jack's. I had a lump in my throat, but I had given Jack my word and now it was payment day. I think Jack knew how I was feeling, but he didn't commiserate or sympathize. He just shook my hand as if I were a man and said, "Johnny, I'm proud of you."

I had a good feeling inside as Dad and I got back in the truck and headed home. I had learned about keeping my word, even when it's hard. As I've grown, I've thanked God many times for this early lesson. Giving up that calf wasn't easy, but it was right. And the sweet memory of Jack's handshake stays with me as a reminder. I always want to have the good feeling of having tried to do right—so God can think, "Johnny, I'm proud of you."

*Dear Lord, You, Who gave up Your life for us, know the tender
sadness of sacrifice. When I need to give something up,
remind me of the sweet pleasure of pleasing You.*
—JOHN COEN, SEPTEMBER 22, 1990

1991

Freedom was in the air this year. In South Africa, apartheid laws were repealed; in Albania, the Communist government resigned; the Soviet-bloc Warsaw Pact was dissolved; Russian Republic president Boris Yeltsin helped to suppress a Communist hard-liner's coup against Soviet President Gorbachev; and the Baltic republics Latvia, Estonia and Lithuania won their independence. On Christmas, following Gorbachev's resignation, the Soviet Union was dissolved.

Popular book titles included *The Secret Pilgrim* by John le Carré, *Cold Fire* by Dean R. Koontz, *The Seeress of Kell* by David Eddings, *Heir to the Empire* by Timothy Zahn, *The Kitchen God's Wife* by Amy Tan, *Iron John* by Robert Bly, *The Prize* by Daniel Yergin, *When You Look Like Your Passport Photo, It's Time to Go Home* by Erma Bombeck, *Uh-Oh* by Robert Fulghum, and *Me: Stories of My Life* by Katharine Hepburn. Moviegoers were frightened by *The Silence of the Lambs,* charmed by *Beauty and the Beast,* and challenged by *JFK* and

Thelma & Louise. On the music charts were "Motownphilly" by Boyz II Men, "Coming Out of the Dark" by Gloria Estefan, "Gonna Make You Sweat" by C + C Music Factory and "Baby Baby" by Amy Grant. A first-class stamp was still twenty-five cents.

In 1991, our fifteenth anniversary year, we offered "Praise," looking at how the apostles model our personal faith journeys in Terry Helwig's "The Twelve in Each of Us" and how we might find answers to our life's concerns in "The Questions Jesus Asked" by Sue Monk Kidd. Newcomer Christopher de Vinck bade us "Come to the Good Shepherd," and Dr. and Mrs. Peale inspired us to find strength in "The Timeless Power of Prayer." Elizabeth Sherrill turned our attention to the Epiphany. We spent Easter week with long-timer Eleanor Sass and Advent with first-timer Scott Walker, learned to deal with illness by "Leaning on the Lord" with Carol Kuykendall and with "C.H.A.N.G.E." with Marilyn Morgan Helleberg.

This year's devotionals are represented by three men. Christopher de Vinck of Pompton Plains, New Jersey, was a high school teacher and administrator and the author of ten books. The one that brought him to our attention was *The Power of the Powerless,* about his brother Oliver, born with multiple severe disabilities. Their mother called Oliver "a gift," and we were privileged to come to know him through Christopher's devotionals.

Scott Harrison, an orthopedic surgeon, was our doctor-in-residence for six years. He and his wife Sally share a great love for Africa, and they've spent many years teaching, healing and helping people all across that continent. Whether he was in a makeshift hospital tending the sick or camping in a tent while on safari, Scott found adventures to share with us.

Daniel Schantz, who is marking his forty-third year of teaching at Central Christian College in Moberly, Missouri, has been a favorite with *Daily Guideposts* readers since he joined us in 1988. A gentle, humble man who writes openly and honestly about his faith, his feelings and his own shortcomings, he seems always able to find the truths in his experiences that will be the most useful for his readers.

Oliver

"Listen! I will unfold a mystery: we shall not all die, but we shall all be changed. . . ."
—I CORINTHIANS 15:51 (NEB)

My brother Oliver was blind, mute, crippled and severely retarded. He lived in our home in a corner of a room with yellow walls, under a window, for his entire life. Each bit of food he ate was brought to his lips by another human being.

One afternoon we were playing in the yard, my brothers and sisters and I, when a friend from school joined us. After an hour of playing ball, Maria, my younger sister who was nine at the time, said to our friend, "You want to see an angel? We got one."

Our schoolmate was curious and skeptical. "Yeah, where?"

Maria led our friend into the house and into Oliver's room. "There. There is our angel."

I do not know what our school friend thought, but I know now, thirty years later, that my sister was right. Oliver was an angel. He was born in April. He never committed a sin. He never grew. He never learned how to speak. Oliver was a baby for thirty-two years.

My mother always said, "Christopher, when you go to Heaven, Oliver will be the first person there to greet you. He will run and dance and laugh."

If you place your hands upon your eyes, if you place your hands upon your lips, if you place your hand upon your beating heart, you will recognize the child that is still in you. The child in you has not died, but has changed. That is the change we are promised after death.

If you visit the Benedictine Monastery in Weston, Vermont, please visit the grave of Oliver, my brother, and place spring flowers upon his grave.

Lord, thank You for the beauty and mystery of life that
You have hidden so purposefully in a child.
—CHRISTOPHER DE VINCK, APRIL 8, 1991

The Strength of the Light

"The Lord is my light and my salvation; whom shall I fear?
—PSALM 27:1

*S*omething was rattling the front door of our hut. When the door shuddered again, my wife Sally bolted out of bed, entangled in her mosquito netting, and frantically thrashed to get free. "What is it?" she gasped.

"Probably a hyena," I said, as my mind raced to think of something to use to defend ourselves. My telephoto camera lens was the largest object I had brought on this weekend of game-viewing in Africa. My pulse raced as I remembered the vicious wounds a woman and her son had recently received from a hyena attack.

Scra-a-ape! Scra-a-ape! It wouldn't be long before our flimsy glass door gave way. There were no electric lights, and I had forgotten a flashlight. As I groped about in the inky blackness, I knocked the candle off the nightstand. It flickered and sputtered as I touched a match to it, then phantom shadows began to dance across the room. I placed the candle by the door and retreated to the back cot with Sally.

Holding each other we began to pray. "Jesus, You are Light. Use this tiny light to drive away this wild beast." We waited in silence, the web of shadows masquerading across the door. The candle burned to exhaustion as dawn reddened the eastern sky. "He's gone," I said, looking out the window. "The light drove him away." But tracks confirmed that a hyena had really been there.

Fortunately, we rarely have wild hyenas trying to devour us. But we do have times when daily stress or difficult problems can trap us in a corner with fear that is very real. When that happens to you, try what worked for Sally and me. Place the Light between you and that which would hurt you. You will find the strength to make it to the dawn.

Lord Jesus, give us Your Light to drive away
the beasts of fear, or sorrow, or....
—SCOTT HARRISON, APRIL 26, 1991

Staying Humble

God hath chosen the weak things of the world to confound
the things which are mighty.
—I CORINTHIANS 1:27

*Y*ou might think a college teacher would feel smart, but not this one. Every day of my twenty-one-year career, I have wrestled with deep feelings of inadequacy.

"It's God's way of keeping you humble," my wife Sharon says.

"But I don't like this feeling."

"Now you know how your students feel. You can sympathize. Besides, you would get lazy and careless if you felt too confident. You would stop studying."

I shrug. "But people think college teachers know everything, and I don't. There's too much to know."

She wraps her arms around me and presses her nose to mine. "Then people will just have to be disappointed."

My worry lines dissolve into a smile. "What's for supper?"

"Don't ask. It's a flop. I can't cook anymore. I feel so inadequate in the kitchen these days."

My turn. "It's God's way of keeping you humble!"

"Get out of here!"

You know, I think Sharon is right. Have you ever thought to thank God for those feelings of inadequacy that keep you trying harder?

Lord, I am weak and needy. I'm trusting You to help me.
—DANIEL SCHANTZ, SEPTEMBER 12, 1991

1992

This year, George Bush and Boris Yeltsin proclaimed a formal end to the Cold War, and Bill Clinton was elected to the presidency.

Millions of TV viewers felt a lump in their throats as Johnny Carson hosted *The Tonight Show* for the last time. We were reading *Hideaway* by Dean R. Koontz, *Rising Sun* by Michael Crichton, *The Pelican Brief* by John Grisham, *Jewels* by Danielle Steel, *Where Is Joe Merchant?* by Jimmy Buffet and *Dolores Claiborne* by Stephen King. In the multiplexes, we could see *Unforgiven, The Crying Game, Howards End, Glengarry Glen Ross* and *The Player.* We listened to "Tears in Heaven" by Eric Clapton, "Constant Craving" by k.d. lang, "Beauty and the Beast" by Celine Dion and Peabo Bryson, "Ain't It Heavy" by Melissa Etheridge and "'Round Midnight" by Bobby McFerrin. A first-class stamp now cost twenty-nine cents.

"Grace" was our theme in *Daily Guideposts, 1992,* and our pages were graced by forty-one writers. Our special features included monthly "Grace Notes" from a variety of authors, a monthly series on relationships from Sue Monk Kidd, and a week of "New Lessons in Faith" from Scott Harrison. We spent Holy Week with Scott Walker and prepared for Christmas with Dr. and Mrs. Peale. And as a special treat, we welcomed twelve readers in "Pathways of Praise," the precursor of today's Reader's Room.

We've chosen three perennial favorites to represent 1992. Kind-hearted, generous and the first to offer help to others, Oscar Greene is also a student of how others live, quick to learn the valuable life lessons they have to teach him—as in this story of his neighbor Casey.

Elizabeth Sherrill has a remarkable talent for finding the spiritual meaning of even the smallest, seemingly inconsequential happenings, such as this noontime concert on a rainy day.

Guideposts' cofounder Ruth Stafford Peale was a truly remarkable woman. A pastor's wife, mother, speaker, administrator and the author of four books, Mrs. Peale maintained a full schedule well into her nineties. Early on, she understood that God had a plan for her life, a plan she learned to trust.

Casey's Strength

Stir up the gift of God, which is in thee....
—II TIMOTHY 1:6

Our neighbor Casey is the strongest person I know.

He used to be a construction worker. Then illness struck—it turned out he had epilepsy. At twenty-three he was out of a job. How could life stop at twenty-three?

That winter Casey noticed that snow removal was a big problem for the many senior citizens in our area, including me. So he began to work at that. Then, as a tool of his new trade, he got quite interested in weather. When storms threatened, he began visiting our homes with his own charts, predicting the storm's path, time of arrival and inches of snow expected. "I listen to twenty-five weather reports a day," he told me.

Casey now has a thriving business: snow removal by winter, lawns and housework by summer, errands all the time. And I have found a new friend. I have enjoyed giving him books on meteorology plus reams of graph paper left over from my engineering days. I've recommended him to new customers too.

Casey's life has turned out quite differently from what he had planned. Life threw a nasty curve at him when he least expected it. Instead of giving up and feeling sorry for himself, he kept going and didn't look back. He "found the gift of God, which was in him," and showed our whole neighborhood that life doesn't have to stop at twenty-three, or forty-three or sixty-three...

Our neighbor Casey is still the strongest person I know.

Gracious Father, when a window closes, it doesn't shut out Your light. It's always there; help us to look for it.
—OSCAR GREENE, JANUARY 29, 1992

Mozart for One

*Are not five sparrows sold for two farthings, and not one of
them is forgotten before God? But even the very hairs of
your head are all numbered . . . ye are of more value than
many sparrows.*

—LUKE 12:6–7

The pouring rain matched my mood. The hospital information
desk where I volunteered one morning a week had only a couple of
inquiries in four hours. With a sense of wasted time I drove through
the sodden streets to attend a noontime concert at our local library.

I left my umbrella at the door . . . and stepped into an empty au-
ditorium. The weather was bad but—was I going to be the only one
here? As the flutist in her long green dress walked onto the stage I
wanted to sink into the floor to spare her this embarrassment.

Following her came a man and a woman. The man sat down at
the piano, while the woman positioned herself behind him to turn the
pages. Surely they weren't going to go ahead with the concert—three
performers before an audience of one! But the flutist, with a little bow,
lifted her gleaming instrument and launched into a Mozart sonata.

At its close I discovered what a disconsolate sound two clapping hands make in an empty room. The flutist bowed again as the pianist set out a second score. The numbers were listed on the mimeographed sheet I'd picked up at the entrance. They played the entire program.

When they finished I went forward to thank them. "To think you played it all for just one person! I wish a thousand had been here!"

The soloist looked at me curiously. *"Just* one person?" she asked. "But...if one person isn't important, how could a thousand be?"

One listener at a concert. One hospital visitor seeking directions. What if totals are a human concept...what if God counts always one by one?

Free me, Father, from bondage to numbers. Let me serve
with gladness the individuals You love.
—ELIZABETH SHERRILL, APRIL 8, 1992

God's Plan and Ours

How unsearchable are his judgments, and
his ways past finding out!
—ROMANS 11:33

*I*n the summer of 1923, my brother Charles Stafford was preparing for his senior year at Syracuse University. But there was a serious problem: money. There had never been much of it in our family. In fact, in later years I realized we were very poor, though our parents never let us feel that way. When it came to financing college educations for my two brothers and me, they were in no position to help.

We had a family conference. At that time I had completed one year at City College in Detroit. The idea was put forward that if I would drop out of college and go to work to help Charles through his senior year, then he would help me for the remaining three years of my schooling.

That was a terrible blow to me. I would lose my friends at school, fall behind one whole year, be forced into a job that didn't promise any fun. But I agreed, and after a year of working in the commercial department of the Michigan Bell Telephone Company, I entered Syracuse University in the fall of 1924.

Why am I telling you this story? It's to underscore something I believe deeply: *God has a plan for my life, even when I am experiencing severe setbacks and can't understand His reasons.*

You see, without that delay I wouldn't have met Norman Vincent Peale. If I had not dropped out of school that year, I would have graduated before Norman arrived at Syracuse to become pastor of the University Methodist Church. No, I simply would not have met him.

One more reason for this story: Today is our sixty-second wedding anniversary.

Dear Lord, we often become impatient and ask, "Why me?"
Help us to know that Your plan will be the right one
for our whole lives. Amen.
—RUTH STAFFORD PEALE, JUNE 20, 1992

1993

In the headlines of 1993, we read about China breaking the nuclear test moratorium, a preliminary Israeli-Palestinian accord and—in a chilling precursor of what was to come—New York's World Trade Center was rocked by a bomb.

Fiction readers devoured *Dragon Tears* by Dean R. Koontz, *The Bridges of Madison County* and *Slow Waltz in Cedar Bend* by Robert James Waller, *The Client* by John Grisham, and *Without Remorse* by Tom Clancy, while nonfiction readers tried Bill Moyers' *Healing and the Mind* and Clarissa Pinkola Estés's *Women Who Run with the Wolves*. Moviegoers watched *Schindler's List*, *The Piano*, *Philadelphia*, *Six Degrees of Separation* and *In the Name of the Father*, while we listened to "I Will Always Love You" by Whitney Houston, "A Whole New World" by Peabo Bryson and Regina Belle, "If I Ever Lose My Faith in You" by Sting, "Another Sad Love Song" by Toni Braxton and

"Passionate Kisses" by Mary Chapin Carpenter. First-class stamps remained at twenty-nine cents.

Three dozen contributors explored "The Gift of Hope" in *Daily Guideposts, 1993*. Elizabeth Sherrill led off with "The Healing Power of Hope," and we had abundant gifts from other members of our family—Phyllis Hobe, Christopher de Vinck, Carol Knapp and Fay Angus all contributed special series. But two of the offerings that year were most notable: In her Holy Week series, "Transformed in the Broken Places," Marilyn Morgan Helleberg (King) broke new ground in dealing honestly and sensitively with the end of her marriage and how sorrow and suffering can give way to healing and joy. And, in October, Sue Monk Kidd said good-bye to *Daily Guideposts* in "Weaving Change into Your Life." But we also said hello to two other Kidds, unrelated to Sue though related to each other: Pam Kidd and her son Brock from Nashville, Tennessee.

During her thirty-three years with *Daily Guideposts*, Marilyn Morgan Helleberg has shared the good times and the tough with *Daily Guideposts* readers. She's written—with deep honesty and sensitivity—of death and grieving, broken friendships and even her own painful divorce. But with the hurts have come many healings, as in the story about her father.

Eric Fellman is the president of the World Bible Translation Center in North Richland Hills, Texas. For many years, Eric worked at the Peale Center for Christian Living, founded by Dr. and Mrs. Peale to advance Christianity as a practical way of life. As its president, he guided the Peale Center's integration into Guideposts as our outreach division. A *Daily Guideposts* contributor since 1988, Eric has written many memorable devotionals about his family adventures with his wife

Joy and their three sons. Here his son Nathan learns the real secret of fishing.

In her fourteen years with *Daily Guideposts*, Sue Monk Kidd had become one of our most prolific and popular contributors. When her journey took a different direction, one that would take her out into the wider world as one of our most acclaimed novelists, she bade good-bye to the *Daily Guideposts* family in the beautiful and poignant devotional we present here.

The Boy My Father Was

He ... healed them that had need of healing.

—LUKE 9:11

*I*n the process of moving, I came across a photograph of my father at age five. I can't tell you how dear that picture has become to me. Though I loved my dad very much, I was really rather scared of him when I was a little girl. Physically, he was a giant of a man, with a quick temper and a loud, stern voice. Life was tough during the Depression years, and it didn't take much to upset this man—a doctor by profession—who carried the concerns of so many sick patients. Though he mellowed a lot in later years, my early memories of his temper still surface now and then.

But the picture I found, with Daddy's name and "age five" written on the back, shows a fragile, vulnerable little boy—the kind you want to pick up and hug and say, "It's okay, honey. I'll take care of you!" I think of how much suffering it took to bring that sensitive boy to the status of tempestuous giant! And though it may not make much sense, I've been strangely moved to pray for my father the little boy, which has led me to the healing of my own spirit—that of the scared little girl.

Maybe you have some childhood pain that needs healing. If you can't find a picture of your parent as a child, just try to visualize her/him as a vulnerable five-year-old child. Then pray for that child. You will be surprised at what happens *within you.*

Heavenly Father, please hold that tender little child
in Your loving arms, healing all the old hurts.
—MARILYN MORGAN HELLEBERG, JUNE 18, 1993

The Fisherman's Secret

And it came to pass, that, while they communed together and
reasoned, Jesus himself drew near, and went with them.

—LUKE 24:15

*D*ad," said thirteen-year-old Nathan, "I think we have the fish outnumbered." I looked about drowsily from under my battered baseball cap to see his scorn-filled look. Gazing out at the spectacular light show the evening sun was projecting across the rippling lake, I breathed deeply of the cool evening breeze and decided to impart some fatherly wisdom.

"Nathan," I said, "I'm going to teach you the secret of fishing." His look said, "Oh yeah?" but I plunged ahead. "You see, son, fishing is not about catching fish. Nope, for me fishing is about getting away for a while, about breathing outdoor air and feeling the sun, about hearing God in the breeze or watching His hand in the clouds. Most of all, it's my excuse to spend some time with you, or with your brothers, or sometimes with all four of us, and building some memories."

It sounded so corny even I laughed, but we talked until dark about nothing and everything. I figured Nathan didn't get my point, until I came across an essay he wrote for a class assignment on *A Summer Memory:* "My summer memory is the afternoon my dad took me fishing and we didn't a catch a thing, but we sat around talking about everything from girls to God, and Dad called it 'building memories.'"

His words reminded me how powerful building memories or communing can really be. Take some time this week to be with someone special. As you share the time together, with or without a set plan, be ready to find Jesus joining you.

Lord, help me find Your presence this week through
spending time with someone I love.
—ERIC FELLMAN, JULY 10, 1993

Setting Sail

I press on toward the goal....
—PHILIPPIANS 3:14 (RSV)

While vacationing in New Mexico, my friend Betty and I hike in Santa Fe National Forest, in a place called Holy Ghost Canyon. We follow a stream that tumbles like a silver ribbon through spruce and quaking aspen, through wild iris and past iridescent hummingbirds.

After a couple of hours we open our backpacks and spread out the picnic we brought along: a loaf of bread, red grapes, some cheese and apple juice. I pull out the tiny basket I made from the scuppernong vines in my backyard, those testy vines I had to soak a while back to make them pliable enough to weave. I'm not exactly sure why I brought it along. I set it on a rock beside the stream and slice some bread into it.

As we eat, I think how the basket has come to represent my own life and the change being woven into it. Beside me, the stream sings over the rocks, moving on, always moving. It reminds me of the flow and passage of life, of yesterdays and todays flowing into tomorrows. And suddenly I know why I brought the little basket all this way to a canyon named Holy Ghost. I place it at the edge of the water and give it a gentle push. I send it off like a prayer. Instantly, it is swept into a current and sails away. I watch it go. I watch until it disappears around a bend. I stand there a long while. After long months of struggle and waiting, something inside of me has set sail.

Today, as I write these words to you, I remember that moment and reimagine the scene by the river. Emotions well up inside me. You, dear readers, and I have traveled together in these pages for such a long time. We've come a long way. And now...well, there are so many feelings I hold. Parting is difficult. And there's so much I could say, but let me try:

Dear Daily Guideposts *friends,*

I am grateful for all the years my life floated your way. Now it floats on. But with a prayer: that whatever blessings may have come to you from my small basket, you will carry them with you always. For I carry your friendship with me around every bend in the stream. God be with you, my friends. Now and always.

Love,

Sue

Dear God, push us gently upon this holy current and sail with us into tomorrow. Amen.

—SUE MONK KIDD, OCTOBER 23, 1993

1994

We were shocked this year to read that Aldrich Ames, a high CIA official, had been charged with spying for Soviets, and to see the Major League Baseball season once again interrupted by a players' strike. And we relived the Watergate era in August when former President Richard Nixon died.

ER and *Friends* debuted on TV, while *Forrest Gump, Pulp Fiction, The Shawshank Redemption, Quiz Show* and *Nobody's Fool* opened in the movie theaters. We read *Disclosure* by Michael Crichton, *Accident* by Danielle Steel, *The Celestine Prophecy* by James Redfield, *Remember Me* by Mary Higgins Clark, *The Chamber* by John Grisham, *The Book of Virtues* by William Bennett, *Barbara Bush: A Memoir,* Pope John Paul II's *Crossing the Threshold of Hope,* and *Politically Correct Bedtime Stories* by James Finn Garner. In the air were the sounds of "I Will Always Love You" by Whitney Houston, "A Whole New World" by Peabo Bryson and Regina Belle, "If I Ever Lose My Faith in You" by Sting,

"Another Sad Love Song" by Toni Braxton and "Passionate Kisses" by Mary Chapin Carpenter. A first-class stamp was still only twenty-nine cents.

In 1994, our *Daily Guideposts* family of thirty-eight celebrated "Prayer: The Mightiest Force in the World." Marilyn Morgan Helleberg provided "Gifts of the Season," short poems and prayers to open every month. Pam Kidd followed with "Prayer Can Change Your Life," in which she told us how the classic book of the same name by Dr. William Parker and Elaine St. Johns had changed hers. Eric Fellman accompanied us through Holy Week and Phyllis Hobe did the same through Advent, and Linda Ching Sledge and her son Timothy, Daniel Schantz, and Elizabeth Sherrill all contributed weeklong series, as did freed Lebanon hostage David Jacobson, who told us how faith had helped him through his ordeal in "Faith: Your Daily Survival Kit." New to our family that year was Dolphus Weary, who continues to inspire us with his work in racial reconciliation and community development in rural Mississippi.

Pam Kidd of Nashville, Tennessee, joined in 1993 and she's been a *Daily Guideposts* favorite ever since. Ever alive to the beauty and wonder of the natural world and the richness and depth of the people around her—as well as their quirks and foibles, not least her own—Pam has allowed us to share in her life as a pastor's wife, a mother (and now a grandmother!), an advocate for the poor and disenfranchised and a part-time Realtor. Here she tells us what God had to say to her one day on her 5:00 AM run.

Dolphus Weary of Richland, Mississippi, lives the meaning of Christian brotherhood with grace, compassion and serenity. Through the REAL Christian Foundation and Mission Mississippi, Dolphus and his wife Rosie have been pioneers of racial reconciliation among churches in his native state and around the country. Here he tells us how a heart for others sometimes takes us out of our comfort zone.

Pam Kidd's son Brock came to us with his mom back in 1993. We've shared his heartaches as well as his triumphs as he's grown to become a successful investment adviser. We've seen him learn the meaning of sacrifice and service and put the lessons he's received from his grandfather and father into raising his own son. And he's shared with us what he's discovered about the things that really matter.

A Run in the Dark

To him that rideth upon the heavens...
lo, he doth send out his voice....
—PSALM 68:33

*I*t's five o'clock on a frosty Tennessee morning. *This timing is ridiculous,* I think as I tug at my gloves and readjust my hand-weights...but it's the only time I have. When I return from my run, my daughter Keri, fifteen, will be getting ready for school and my husband David will most likely be in the kitchen grinding beans for coffee. We'll talk as I pack Keri's lunch and later we'll snatch a few minutes together over breakfast before we go our separate ways for the long day ahead.

Out on the street, it's as dark as midnight. I don't see the moon, but everywhere there are stars. As I run my familiar course, I glance up into the heavens. "Look at that," I say out loud, "the Big Dipper's still there."

As I continue on, I chuckle at the sound of my unexpected words breaking through the silence of the cold morning, but they've set me thinking. Life seems to rush by so fast. There's always too much to do in too little time. But the Big Dipper's still there, just as it was when I was four and fourteen and twenty-four. Something to depend on. Like God Who waits for us to look...to see...to feel His presence.

I round the block and head back home. Before I go inside, I stand and look at the sky. I don't feel so rushed now. In fact, I feel fit and energized, ready for anything. Sure, the day will stretch out long and busy, but I intend to remember my morning words and to remind myself often of the truth they have revealed: *The Big Dipper's still there...and so is God.*

In a world ever-changing, God, let me focus on
Your never-changing presence.
—PAM KIDD, FEBRUARY 15, 1994

Hoop Dreams

"For where you go I will go, and where you lodge I will lodge;
your people shall be my people, and your God my God."
—RUTH 1:16 (RSV)

When I was growing up in the country, I learned how to play basketball by shooting a tin can into a bucket. It wasn't until I was in high school that I got my first basketball and a rim to go with it. As soon as I nailed the rim to the tree, kids from all around came over to play. When my son Reggie was nine, he asked, "Dad, can you put a basketball hoop in our backyard?"

"No," I said. "I don't want our yard to become the neighborhood playground." It would have been the only hoop in the community. I guess I liked my peace and quiet.

But God began working on me through my wife Rosie. "What's a little bit of grass and a quiet Saturday morning when we can offer the children a chance to have fun?" she asked me. Finally, a year later, we put up a hoop. And guess what? Our yard was immediately full of kids.

Then, and at other times, I have wondered why we stay in a poor community. Almost every day there is a new crisis on our street or the next one over. I see children who go without, parents who work all night in a factory and people who struggle under the burden of poverty.

"We are here because God has called us to be *a part of,* not apart from, this community," Rosie says thoughtfully, wisely. "We are called to share the problems. When the creek spills over its banks, our house is flooded too. We are called to look for the solutions together. And we are called to share ourselves and our resources."

Now when I pass the gym that our ministry helped build in our community—and play some ball myself—I'm glad I put up that first hoop. It confronted me with the needs of the young people and made me look for better solutions. The gym was one. And I look at the children around me and thank God for the privilege of lodging among them.

Our precious Savior, thank You for coming to earth to lodge among us. Help me to continue to follow Your example.
—DOLPHUS WEARY, JUNE 16, 1994

The Car That Wasn't

"He will turn ... the hearts of children to their fathers. ...."
—MALACHI 4:6 (RSV)

rock," my dad begins as he casts his line out onto the mirrored surface of Lake Weiss. It's late afternoon and we are out in the little red fishing boat that Mom bought a few years ago, thinking to surprise us. "About the car," Dad continues as he reels his line back.

I knew that my parents had hoped to help me buy a car by my junior year in college. Hitching rides back and forth to school was getting more difficult, and working part-time off-campus with no transportation was a pain. But summer was almost over, and I knew the car wasn't to be. It had been a summer of unexpected expenses. Medical and dental bills, car repairs (our family's newest car had more than a hundred thousand miles on it), a broken water heater one month, a broken air conditioner the next. August was here, and the savings account held just enough to get me back in school. No more.

So here we were, Mom, Dad, Keri and I, spending a few vacation days at a cabin in Leesburg, Alabama. None of us had mentioned the car till now.

Long ago, my father made the choice to give his life to God. Being a minister has brought a lot of rewards, but a huge salary is not one of them. Sometimes it's hard to see Dad rejoicing when others describe their fancy vacations, country homes and their two cars. It's hard because I know how much he would love to give us those things...how much it hurts because he can't.

"Dad," I answer, looking out on the horizon where the sun is just beginning to set, "remember when Mom bought us this boat, she was so proud that she got it for a hundred dollars." We laughed, remembering our first horrified glimpse of the strange, too-small, too-slow boat, which Dad teasingly named Thunder. "A big fancy bass boat couldn't ever replace the good times we've had in old Thunder. You know, Dad, there are lots of things more important than a car. Some of them you can't buy. Why, I wouldn't trade this time with you for any car in the world," I say.

I hope he understands. Because I have spoken the truth.

God, help us to never lose sight of the things in our lives
that really matter the most. Amen.
—BROCK KIDD, AUGUST 27, 1994

1995

In the headlines this year, Americans visited the Russian space station *Mir* for the first time, Israeli Prime Minister Yitzhak Rabin was slain at a peace rally, and a Los Angeles jury found O. J. Simpson not guilty of murder charges.

The books we were reading included *Beach Music* by Pat Conroy, *From Potter's Field* by Patricia Cornwell, *"L" Is for Lawless* by Sue Grafton, *The Horse Whisperer* by Nicholas Evans, *The Lost World* by Michael Crichton, *The Christmas Box* by Richard Paul Evans, *The Hot Zone* by Richard Preston, *Breaking the Surface* by Greg Louganis and Colin Powell's *My American Journey*. The movies that got us into the theaters included *Babe, Braveheart, Leaving Las Vegas, The Usual Suspects* and *Dead Man Walking*. The song hits included "Kiss from a Rose" by Seal, "You Oughta Know" by Alanis Morrisette, "You Don't Know How It Feels" by Tom Petty, "For Your Love" by Stevie Wonder and "Baby, Now That I've Found You" by Alison Krauss. And the Rock and Roll Hall of Fame opened in Cleveland. On the first of the year, the price of a first-class stamp climbed to thirty-two cents.

Our 1995 theme was "Looking Ahead: The Bright and Positive Side of Change." Joining us that year among our forty-four writers were Lurlene McDaniel, who contributed a touching series on her fight against breast cancer, Susan Schefflein, and Bill Irwin, who hiked the Appalachian Trail with his Seeing Eye dog. Elizabeth Sherrill helped us in "Facing the Unknown Future"; Sandra Simpson LeSourd told us how her struggles with addiction and failure pointed her "Toward Easter's Joy." We gathered "Around the Campfire" with Mary Lou Carney, went on "Adventures in the Yukon" with Carol Knapp, worked on "Building a Friendship" with Linda Ching Sledge and looked toward Christmas with *Daily Guideposts* editor Mary Ruth Howes. And in devotionals by Arthur Gordon and Ruth Stafford Peale, we celebrated Guideposts' fiftieth anniversary.

Dr. Norman Vincent Peale passed away at the age of ninety-five on Christmas Eve 1993. A year later, Mrs. Peale shared a word of encouragement she'd found in the pages of *Daily Guideposts*.

While most *Daily Guideposts* devotionals are first-person stories, sometimes our writers break out of that mold. Daniel Schantz, for example, often writes devotionals in the form of prayers. He isn't afraid to share his sorrows, regrets, doubts or misgivings. And his honesty has helped us all over the rough places in our own roads.

Marion Bond West would be the first to admit that her prayers are often full of questions—*How, God? Why? What? When?*—cries for help, for release, for comfort. "I need..." prayers, she calls them. In the devotional here, though, she discovers the power of another kind of prayer entirely.

A Peaceful Passing

*Whatsoever is born of God overcometh the world: and this is
the victory that overcometh the world, even our faith.*

—I JOHN 5:4

As I write this for January 24, 1995, it is exactly one year and one month to the day when my husband Norman Vincent Peale passed away. His passing was very peaceful on Christmas Eve. He was surrounded by family and loved ones, and we stood in a circle by his bed as our wonderful physician, Dr. Milnor M. Morrison, led us in prayer. We were giving Norman back to God.

In time I went to the kitchen, made myself a cup of tea, sat down with an earlier edition of *Daily Guideposts* and reread some of its messages at random. I came across a devotional by Eric Fellman in which he told about the last Little League baseball game of the season when the team he coached lost by one point. Tears were near the surface in the boys' eyes. "Boys," Eric said, "losing doesn't make you losers. Acting beaten makes you a loser." Hope came to the boys and one shouted, "Mr. Fellman, are you going to coach us next year?" The answer was yes.

In a way, it's odd that a story about a kids' baseball team would be helpful at this moment, but I found myself saying, "Ruth, don't act like a loser. Think of yourself as a winner. Keep on working just as you and Norman always did. That's the positive thing to do!"

And from that moment to this one, I have been firm in this belief: No one should lose to loss.

Thank You, Lord Jesus, that in all our defeats
You show us victory.
—RUTH STAFFORD PEALE, JANUARY 24, 1995

In His Presence

The heart knows its own bitterness,
And a stranger does not share its joy.
—PROVERBS 14:10 (NKJV)

 Lord,

I've been so lonely today. And with no apparent cause. You've given me a wonderful wife, two beautiful daughters and a precious grand-baby. I still have my mom and dad, who gave me three brothers and two sisters, and now I have lots of nephews and nieces. I have dozens of students who look up to me and make me laugh a lot. Plus friends all over town and in forty states. Yet, still, I'm lonely. I feel as though no one else in the world could ever understand this emptiness. It really hurts.

Remember when I was younger, I used to run from this feeling? I'd go to parties or work till late at night or watch TV marathon-style. But I'm older now. And I know those things don't really fill the loneliness.

So, today, instead of running away and trying to deaden this ache, I sat down and wrote in my journal in an effort to put a name to my feelings. You know, of course, what I wrote—that I've turned loneliness into a friend, someone who is trying to reacquaint me with the only One Who truly understands what I am feeling. Now I see that I have a thirst that only You can satisfy. I have an itch that only You can salve.

So here I am, Lord.

Your loving son,

Dan

—DANIEL SCHANTZ, FEBRUARY 11, 1995

John Henry's Prayer

It is a good thing to give thanks unto the Lord. . . .
—PSALM 92:1

*J*ohn Henry Maddox takes wonderful care of our yard. He cuts
the grass, weeds the flowerbeds and plants shrubs. He and our yard
are buddies. Sometimes when John Henry's near our home, he stops
by just to check on "his" yard. He tells my husband Gene marvelous
hints such as, "You put out tomato plants with Epsom salts around
the roots."

John Henry prefers to eat out on the back porch, even in hot
weather. He doesn't like air conditioning. One day, I served him lunch
on the porch and then went back inside and actually forgot that he was
out there. Suddenly I heard this powerful voice, loudly calling, "God!"
Was John Henry hurt? I hurried outside and stopped in the doorway.

I had forgotten for a moment that John Henry was deaf and sometimes speaks louder than is necessary. His pre-lunch blessing was loud
enough for the entire neighborhood to hear. It wasn't a short or matter-
of-fact blessing. It was a prayer by a man who was intimately acquainted with God. I bowed my head until the lengthy prayer was

finished. "...And thank You for the food, for my good health, for my friends Gene and Marion, and for the opportunity to care for *our* yard."

Back inside, I went to a chair where I like to pray and began to offer my thanks to the Lord...for John Henry, for a yard, a home, a husband, our church, our health, the good news that had come in the mail...

Lord, so often my "I need" prayers are more frequent and intense than my "thank You" prayers. Teach me how to reverse that order. Amen.

—MARION BOND WEST, JULY 27, 1995

1996

In 1996, Madeleine Albright became our first female Secretary of State, and Britain was alarmed by an outbreak of "mad cow" disease. Of the 43.2 million (44 percent) of US households with a personal computer, fourteen million of them were online.

Notable books this year included *It Takes a* Village by Hillary Rodham Clinton, *The Dilbert Principle* by Scott Adams, *Angela's Ashes* by Frank McCourt, *Intensity* by Dean R. Koontz, *Primary Colors* by Anonymous (Joe Klein), *How Stella Got Her Groove Back* by Terry McMillan, *The Runaway Jury* by John Grisham, *Cause of Death* by Patricia Cornwell and *The Deep End of the Ocean* by Jacquelyn Mitchard. We watched *The English Patient, Fargo, Jerry Maguire, Shine* and *Sling Blade*. We listened to "Change the World" by Eric Clapton, "Falling into You" by Celine Dion, "If It Makes You Happy" by Sheryl Crow and "Bullet with Butterfly Wings" by the Smashing Pumpkins. And we mourned the passing of one of the great figures of American popular song, jazz great Ella Fitzgerald. We were still paying thirty-two cents for a first-class stamp.

The theme of our twentieth edition was "Lights in the Darkness," and our fifty-one writers included some exciting new lights: the noted children's writer Katherine Paterson visited us for a year, while then *Guideposts* senior editor (now editor-in-chief) Edward Grinnan, nurse Roberta Messner, prolific Christian writer Keith Miller (who gave us our Holy Week series), and then Guideposts book division editor-in-chief Brigitte Weeks became permanent parts of the family. Pam Kidd took us through Advent in a "Journey toward the Light," while Elizabeth Sherrill told us monthly about "My Gift Today." We've chosen three devotionals to represent that anniversary year.

Keith Miller is the author of more than two dozen books, including such classics as *Habitation of Dragons* and *A Taste of New Wine*. As a speaker, writer and counselor, Keith has helped thousands of people find release from longstanding burdens and fears—because, as here, he's so unflinchingly shared his struggles with his own.

John Sherrill and his wife and writing partner Elizabeth (Tib) met aboard a ship on their way to Europe and were married in Switzerland in 1947. They've been part of the Guideposts family for more than fifty years, and among our most-loved devotional writers since *Daily Guideposts'* third year. Like Tib, John has an uncanny ability to the see the message God is sending in almost any situation and an unrivaled skill in telling a story.

Phyllis Hobe lived in the country in Greenville, Pennsylvania, with plenty of open space for her family of pets: Suzy, a Rottweiler; Kate, a German shepherd; and Mr. Jones, her cat. She often wrote about her encounters with the animals she loved: birds, deer, rabbits and, above all, her cat and dogs.

The Power of the Powerless

But he said to me, "My grace is sufficient for you,
for my power is made perfect in weakness."
—II CORINTHIANS 12:9 (RSV)

A few years ago, I went into the hospital to have a bladder examination for a suspected malignancy. After the exam, the urologist said, "Well, Keith, there's good news and bad news. The good news is that you don't have cancer." He paused.

"What's the bad news?" I asked quickly.

"The bad news is that you have an incurable disease called interstitial cystitis. But if you can learn to live one day at a time and follow the prescribed diet and exercise program, you may be able to keep this from getting worse."

"What happens if I don't respond?"

"Well," he said, "ultimately it could be fatal."

I went home feeling very helpless, angry and afraid. I've always hated not being in control of my life. But when I prayed that day, I got the clear sense that God was telling me, "I have some things for you to do, and I want you to get about doing them."

So I began a journey of *having* to trust God one day at a time in my weakness. I did exactly what the doctor said about diet and exercise. Each morning I would surrender my powerlessness, my life and the disease to God. Then, paradoxically, I began to feel free and clearheaded. Although I felt powerless over the disease, I felt a different kind of power that enabled me to accomplish a number of creative projects.

A year later, I went back to the doctor for a checkup. At the conclusion of the examination, he said, "I can't find any evidence that you still have the disease. You may be the first person who has been cured of it."

As I drove home, I could hear Jesus telling me again to follow His example to love and serve others, to do God's will, not my own (John 6:38; 13:14–16). I don't know what tomorrow will bring, but I now know that I am not to control the outcome of my life. I am to live for God one day at a time.

Lord, Your strength grows out of my admission of powerlessness.
Help me to keep trusting Your love and care.
—KEITH MILLER, APRIL 13, 1996

Time to Prepare

I will therefore now make preparation for it.
—I CHRONICLES 22:5

I was a college sophomore when I was called into the US Army to fight in World War II. I was sent to Camp Wolters, Texas, where on the very first day, in 110-degree heat, we were marched to the parade ground to learn close-order drill.

Sergeant McElwain, heavyset and red of face, barked out orders. "Ri-i-i-ight, face!" After being chewed out a few times, we learned never to move on the word *Ri-i-i-ight*, but only on the word *face*.

I soon discovered that Sergeant McElwain was following a time-tested pattern for giving an order. First comes the slow, drawn out "preparation command" after which the officer snaps the "command of execution."

I have since found this same sequence often applies to my ongoing walk with God: A long period when nothing seems to happen is followed by a sudden rush of activity. I remember how, years ago, my wife Tib and I had run out of living space in our small starter home. The baby slept next to the laundry machine; the garage was full of bikes and boxes; our bedroom doubled as an office. Clearly, it was time to move. We began looking for a new home, but in spite of our continuing prayers, nothing showed up. An entire year passed. Two. And still we saw nothing we liked or could afford.

Then one day a neighbor told us about a house that had just come on the market. It had exactly the number of rooms we needed; it had woods, a brook, two fireplaces. Tib walked around the house in one direction; I walked around it the other way. We met in the front yard, nodded and threw our arms around each other.

The long preparation command had been followed by an abrupt command of execution. Now we acted in a hurry. Within one week we agreed on terms, and we have been happy in our home for more than thirty-seven years.

Lord, how I appreciate Your preparing my heart and mind
for the things You have in store for me to do.
—JOHN SHERRILL, AUGUST 12, 1996

Making Friends

If we walk in the light, as he is in the light,
we have fellowship one with another....
—I JOHN 1:7

*W*hen people who don't know me see me walking my dog Suzy, they often go the other way. Suzy is a rottweiler, weighs more than one hundred pounds and, as a friend put it, "looks very intimidating." Actually, she's a giant puppy with a loving disposition, but not many people want to get close enough to find that out.

Not long after I got Suzy, on our morning walks we began to meet a woman walking her golden retriever. We both pulled our dogs in close to our sides, and as they passed each other, the fur on their backs went up. That bothered me because that wasn't like the Suzy I knew. So I decided to take a bit of a risk. The next morning, as my neighbor and her dog approached, I stopped, put Suzy on a "sit" command and asked, "Do you think it might be a good idea for our dogs to get to know each other?"

The woman smiled and said, "I certainly do."

The dogs got along wonderfully, and so did their two owners. Now all four of us look forward to our morning meetings.

Every now and then I come across people who intimidate me because they seem to be more confident and capable than I am, so I make no attempt to know them better. I stick to my own side of the road. But the next time I feel intimidated, I'm going to take a risk. I'm going to say hello and hold out my hand. I might discover someone who's just like me—a person. And instead of making a fool of myself, I might make a friend.

Father, help me not to let fear and imagination keep me
from seeing people as they really are.
—PHYLLIS HOBE, AUGUST 20, 1996

1997

In the papers and newscasts this year, we learned about new scientific cooperation between Russia and the US as our space shuttle joined the Russian space station. Timothy J. McVeigh was sentenced to death for the Oklahoma City bombing, and Princess Diana died tragically in a Paris car crash, mourned by millions around the world.

On our nightstands were such books as Billy Graham's *Just As I Am*, John Krakuers' *Into Thin Air*, *Underboss* by Pete Maas, *Hornet's Nest* and *Unnatural Exposure* by Patricia Cornwell, *The Partner* by John Grisham, *Plum Island* by Nelson DeMille and *Cold Mountain* by Charles Frazier. Movie theaters featured *As Good As It Gets*, *The Full Monty*, *Good Will Hunting*, *The Ice Storm*, *L.A. Confidential* and *Titanic*, then the most expensive motion picture of all time. On our Walkmans and radios we listened to "Sonny Came Home" by Shawn Colvin, "Building a Mystery" by Sarah McLachlan, "Don't Look Back" by John Lee Hooker and Van Morrison, "Criminal" by Fiona

Apple, "I Believe I Can Fly" by R. Kelly. We still paid thirty-two cents to mail a letter.

Daily Guideposts turned twenty-one this year with a focus on "The Wonder of God's Love." We welcomed a bumper crop of new voices to our chorus of forty-six: Kjerstin Easton (now Williams), then a freshman at Caltech; Mark Collins, a fresh voice from Pittsburgh, Pennsylvania; Roberta Rogers; Julia Attaway and her husband Andrew, the new editor of *Daily Guideposts*. Our special series were from Elizabeth Sherrill ("Love Is...," based on Paul's great hymn to love in I Corinthians 13); Marilyn Morgan Helleberg, imagining herself following Jesus through the events of Holy Week; Eric Fellman on "The Candles of Christmas"; Mary Lou Carney and Carol Kuykendall.

Marion Bond West has always been willing to share her deepest fears and her most profound encounters with God. In her 1997 devotional, she confronts a loved one's dreaded diagnosis and a most remarkable dream.

Since she and her husband Andrew joined the *Daily Guideposts* family just two years after their wedding, we've watched Julia Attaway's family (now five children strong)—and her faith—grow and blossom. In this devotional from her first year, she takes us back to that family's beginning.

Patricia Lorenz came to us in 1987 from Oak Park, Wisconsin, as a single mother (two daughters and two sons) and the consummate professional writer—she's written eleven books and more than four hundred articles—who can, with equal facility, give us a chuckle, start a tear or pass on a down-to-earth tip for living. Here she shares a long-ago memory as sweet as a root beer float.

In His Arms

In His arm he will gather the lambs....

—ISAIAH 40:11 (NAS)

The call we'd been waiting for came at seven on a May evening while I sat on my mother's front porch with my husband Gene. Out of earshot of my mother, I answered the portable phone.

"Marion..." The doctor's voice seemed heavy—determined. Cars passed by Mother's house. Neighbors talked in the yard. A bird sang a late afternoon song. I wanted to throw the phone into the bushes. "Your mother's scan shows what I suspected. The breast cancer from ten years ago has returned in her spine."

Gene and I sat motionless and silent for a few moments as though the call hadn't come. Then I made myself go inside and tell my mother. She didn't seem surprised or terribly alarmed.

We were spending the night, and we all got ready for bed routinely. But once I was in bed, the what-ifs that had tormented me twelve years ago, when my first husband Jerry had brain surgery for cancer, struck without warning. The night was unbelievably long and sleep never came. The sky was becoming light when I realized that I hadn't talked with God about this news.

I'm not angry, Lord. It's just that I didn't expect to have to do it again. I don't know if I can. I feel very far away from You.

Sleep came for perhaps fifteen minutes. In a vivid dream, someone approached me from behind and lifted me as though I were a child. *What powerful arms,* I thought. At first, I believed it was Gene. But this person was incredibly strong and so tall I couldn't even see his face as I rested my head against him. He carried me effortlessly.

Oh, Father, I forgot how strong Your arms are! Amen.
—MARION BOND WEST, JANUARY 14, 1997

Together on the Road

If we are to share his glory, we must also share his suffering.
—ROMANS 8:17 (TLB)

From the very beginning, Andrew was certain we should get married. I sure wasn't! I was the paragon of caution: We'd been seeing each other regularly for months before I'd even concede that we were dating. I warned him repeatedly that he shouldn't hope too much, and that he certainly shouldn't expect me to be ready too soon.

Then New Year's Eve rolled around. After I'd cooked a special dinner, Andrew leaned back and said, "I don't know what I'm going to do if you don't marry me."

I smiled at him in the candlelight and replied, "Well, you haven't asked me lately." Surprised, he asked. I said yes.

As sometimes happens, however, there were a few seeds of worry left in my heart. After the excitement of sharing the happy news of our engagement wore off, my worries slowly took new root. Unbeknownst to Andrew, within a few months they were in full blossom. And so it was that one evening after we'd had a minor spat, I burst into copious and unexpected tears.

"I don't know if we should get married!" I wailed. "What if we don't get along? What if ten years down the road we get on each other's nerves? What if…?" My voice trailed off as anxiety about the future tightened my throat.

Andrew was quiet for a minute. Then he took my hand. "Julia," he said slowly, "there's one thing you can be sure of. If we are meant to walk this road together, there must be a cross on it somewhere."

I married him. It was the best decision of my life.

Lord Jesus, only by walking with You on the road to Calvary can we arrive at Easter Day. Help me to remember that every trouble can bring me closer to You, if only I let it.
—JULIA ATTAWAY, FEBRUARY 21, 1997

A Gift of Belonging

Children are a gift from God; they are his reward.
—PSALM 127:3 (TLB)

One Saturday night, when I was about seven years old, I'd gone to bed at my usual time, eight or eight-thirty. By nine-thirty, I was into a deep, sound sleep.

"Pat, wake up," Dad whispered as he shook my shoulder. "Are you awake? We want you to come out to the kitchen."

"Huh? Why, Daddy?"

"Your mom and I decided to have root beer floats, and we don't want you to miss out. Come on, honey. There's a big 'brown cow' out there for you."

I padded to the kitchen in my big, pink, fluffy slippers and plopped down next to Mom at the old wooden table. I watched Dad scoop the vanilla ice cream into the blue, brown and yellow mugs that had been in my mother's family when she was a girl. The foam from the root beer tickled my nose as I chatted with my folks about school and our family plans for the coming holiday season.

I never felt more loved than I did that night in the kitchen as I groggily slurped root beer and ice cream with my parents. Why? Because Mom and Dad wanted my company enough to wake me up so I could be there. That one simple act did more for my self-esteem than anything I can remember before or since.

Today, Lord, help me to think of a way to do something special for my child, grandchild or young neighbor.
—PATRICIA LORENZ, NOVEMBER 8, 1997

1998

At home, President Clinton was embroiled in a White House sex scandal involving intern Monica Lewinsky. An estimated 76 million viewers watched the last episode of the sitcom *Seinfeld*, while *Titanic*, the highest-grossing film of all time, captured a record-tying eleven Oscars, including Best Picture and Best Director.

When we could pry our eyes off the screen, we read *Paradise* by Toni Morrison, *"N" Is for Noose* by Sue Grafton, *I Know This Much Is True* by Wally Lamb, *The Path of Daggers* by Robert Jordan, *A Man in Full* by Tom Wolfe, *Tuesdays with Morrie* by Mitch Albom, *The Century* by Peter Jennings and Todd Brewster, and Tom Brokaw's *The Greatest Generation*. New in the movie theaters were *Affliction*, *American History X*, *Elizabeth*, *Shakespeare in Love* and *There's Something about Mary*. Song hits included "My Heart Will Go On" (theme from *Titanic*) by Celine Dion, "My Father's Eyes" by Eric Clapton, "Jump, Jive, an' Wail" by the Brian Setzer Orchestra, "Pink" by Aerosmith and "Doo Wop (That Thing)" by Lauryn Hill. And we were still paying thirty-two cents for that first-class stamp.

Our fifty-three contributors to *Daily Guideposts, 1998* focused on "God's Healing Touch." Our first-of-the-month series featured stories of "The Touch of the Healer"; we made a "Journey to Healing" with Scott Harrison and spent Holy Week with Rick Hamlin. Mary Lou Carney found healing for grief in "My Mother's House," and John Sherrill helped us toward "Healing the Fear of Old Age." And at Advent and Christmas, Marion Bond West took us back to six healing Christmases in her life. Visiting us this year were Bill and Kathy Peel of Nashville, Tennessee, while Rhoda Blecker, then a Californian and now of Bellingham, Washington, settled in for a long stay.

A resident of Sierra Madre, California, Fay Angus was born in Brisbane, Australia, raised in Shanghai, China, and spent two and a half years in a Japanese internment camp during World War II, a story she told in her book *The White Pagoda*. Through her devotionals, we've come to know her as a wise mother and a doting grandmother. We've mourned with her for her beloved husband John and, as in the devotional we present here, shared her love for the Savior Who can bear all our pain.

Kjerstin Easton (now Kjerstin Williams), another Californian, came to us as a freshman at Caltech, where she's since gone on to receive a PhD. Kjerstin has brought us a keen eye for God's presence in our lives, as in this devotional about sin, forgiveness and a remarkable plant.

Arthur Gordon always had an acute awareness of the beauty and wonder of the natural world. Here sun, sky and sea provide the stage for a most remarkable ballet.

At the Foot of the Cross

Surely he hath borne our griefs,
and carried our sorrows...

—ISAIAH 53:4

Following a tradition started by a group of brethren in the Taize Community in France, on Good Friday our pastor lays a rough-hewn, life-sized cross flat on the platform in the church sanctuary. Around the cross, beside small kneeling cushions, he places little yellow sticky notes, each with a pencil. From six in the morning until six that evening, our church is open to anyone who would care to come and lay whatever pain they have in their hearts upon the cross.

For a good part of my life, I have carried a pain that will not go away. It woke me in the middle of the night and twisted me up with grief for my father, for all that was and all that could have been. It is a pain I cannot change. "I'll never divorce," my mother said, and she didn't. Instead, I lived with her in a faraway separation from a daddy I adored.

"I'll come to see you," he promised. Week after week in years of broken promises, he never came. Then he died.

Kneeling at the cross, I wrote my pain on a yellow sticky note and gave it to my suffering Lord. The pain did not go away, but it became an okay pain, because now Christ was carrying it for me.

Lord Jesus, take all those things that twist me up with hurt.
I lay them at the foot of Your cross.
—FAY ANGUS, APRIL 1, 1998

The Jericho Rose

He saved us through the washing of rebirth and
renewal by the Holy Spirit.
—TITUS 3:5 (NIV)

*H*ave you ever seen a Jericho rose? It looks like a balled-up fist
or a small tumbleweed, dry and brittle as a closed mind. Its spindly,
tightly curled branches wear the mask of death, and its tiny bundle
of roots seems hardly enough to have held it in place anywhere at all.
The Jericho rose seems to be the sun-baked corpse of a desert weed.

A friend of mine brought one of these pitiful plants to my house
one afternoon. She fished it out of her handbag as I started making
tea. We had planned to prepare for the next week's Bible study and I
remembered her suggestion of baptism or forgiveness of sins as a topic,
but I couldn't see how a lifeless, potless runt of a shrub had anything
to do with it. Smiling, she excavated a shallow bowl, which she filled
with tap water and set on the dining-room table. Extremely curious by
now, I started to ask what she had in mind, but she simply sat down
and looked at the plant. Ever so slowly, its limbs began to straighten

and unfurl. I forgot the tea as I watched the scraggly little branches spread. And was it becoming just a little bit greener?

Fifteen minutes later, the teapot was whistling insistently. The Jericho rose was unfurled now, and I understood its role in the upcoming Bible study. This is my freshman year in college, and the hectic race often leaves me feeling spent and exhausted. It's all too easy for me to neglect to set aside quiet time for prayer and worship. My faith can get as dry and shriveled as a desert plant. But within it are the seeds of life, and by His forgiving grace, God will awaken it, as His gift of water awakens the Jericho rose.

Lord and Giver of life, in the dry times,
help me to remember the Jericho rose.
—KJERSTIN EASTON, APRIL 16, 1998

Morning with Dolphins

These see the works of the Lord, and his wonders in the deep.

—PSALM 107:24

The friends who invited us for a boat ride in their handsome cruiser had also invited three nuns, Sisters of Mercy, who worked at one of our local hospitals. It was a sparkling summer morning, sea almost calm, sky a bottomless blue, gulls drifting by on the silver streaming the wind.

I was sitting up in the bow, talking with one of the sisters, when suddenly about a quarter mile away two streamlined shapes rose out of the sea, arched over in perfect unison high above the water and then disappeared with barely a splash. Dolphins. Big, seven-foot dolphins—good-natured, playful clowns of the sea.

A moment later they leaped again, still in perfect tandem, still racing toward us, almost as if they were saying, "Hey, look at us! We're here, too, you know, in this wonderful world!"

The third leap was so close that we could see their merry eyes watching us, mouths smiling as always, the grace and precision and power of their ballet so effortless and amazing that one felt like applauding.

Down they came in a swirl of green and gold, and were gone. Sister Mary Frances looked at me, eyes wide, and said the only thing there was to say: "Praise the Lord!"

And I murmured, "Amen!"

Thank You, Father, for those flashing moments when we know
that because we are all Your creatures, we are all kin
to one another.
—ARTHUR GORDON, AUGUST 20, 1998

1999

The new year of 1999 saw the birth of a new currency, as the euro was introduced to world financial markets. The US Senate opened its impeachment trial of President Clinton and later acquitted him and rejected a censure move. In Littleton, Colorado, students Eric Harris and Dylan Klebold stormed Columbine High School, killing twelve other students, a teacher and then themselves. As the year ended, the world awaited the consequences of the vaunted "Y2K bug."

Readers on both sides of the Atlantic were wild about Harry— J. K. Rowling's Harry Potter. *Harry Potter and the Sorcerer's Stone*, which first appeared in the US in 1998 but reached the best-seller lists in 1999, *Harry Potter and the Chamber of Secrets*, and *Harry Potter and the Prisoner of Azkaban*. At the movies, we watched *The Blair Witch Project*, *American Beauty*, *Three Kings* and *The Sixth Sense*. We danced to "Smooth" by Santana with Rob Thomas, "I Will Remember You" by Sarah McLachlan, "Brand New Day" by Sting, "Believe" by Cher, and "Scar Tissue" by Red Hot Chili Peppers. As of January, the price of a first-class stamp had risen to thirty-three cents.

As we peered ahead toward a new millennium, *Daily Guideposts* took its theme from the Twenty-third Psalm: "He Leadeth Me." Fifty-two writers joined us, among them newcomers Libbie Adams, Melody Bonnette, Helen Grace Lescheid, Allison Sample and Gail Thorell Schilling. Also new this year was "The Reader's Room," where we welcomed readers' comments and stories. Leading us ahead again was Elizabeth Sherrill, who shared "Lessons in Listening." Isabel Wolseley contributed a series about the weekly routines of her growing-up years. In Holy Week, Shari Smyth told us about her struggle to save the daughter she loves. Eric Fellman shared a time of personal decision in "A Fork in the Road," while Julia Attaway led us through Advent on "The Paths of Christmas."

Mary Jane Clark, her husband Harry and their family lived in the hills of Durango, Colorado. Mary Jane, then a widow, met and married Harry while they were both working in Kenya. Mary Jane received many gifts in Africa, one of which she shares in her devotional here.

Our other 1999 devotionals come from the end of the year: Julia Attaway tells us how a toddler's illness gave her a new appreciation of the truth of Christmas, and Daniel Schantz's New Year's Eve prayer pointed the way to peace in a moment of uncertainty.

The Cave of Winds

And suddenly a sound came from heaven
like the rush of a mighty wind....
—ACTS 2:7 (RSV)

About thirty miles north of Nairobi, Kenya, is a small community called Kijabe, the Place of the Winds. It is perched on the escarpment wall overlooking the Great Rift Valley. When I lived in East Africa, one of my assignments was to write about the work at the mission hospital there for donors in the United States. The views from Kijabe are extraordinary, and I always enjoyed my visits there.

One afternoon the nursing director and I were trying to concentrate on a quiet task together when the wind became particularly gusty, blowing our papers around. "Wind can be so unsettling," I remarked as Norma got up to close the windows.

"Yes, but I think maybe that's its job here on earth—to rearrange things," she replied. With the windows closed we were nearly oblivious to the wind. It howled around the buildings as we carried on with our task.

Later, thinking about what Norma had said, I remembered how the Holy Spirit came with the sound of the wind at Pentecost. The Spirit came to rearrange people's lives, changing their priorities and reordering history. For the people who were there, nothing was ever the same again.

Am I open to that Power in my life? Or do I close my soul up tight at the prospect of change? Am I willing to let God the Holy Spirit blow out the cobwebs and reorder my comfortable routines?

Holy Spirit, I want to keep open the windows of my heart and
let You rearrange my thinking and my doing.
—MARY JANE CLARK, MAY 23, 1999

The Greatest Gift

And the Word was made flesh, and dwelt among us. . . .
—JOHN 1:14

I'm finding it hard to prepare for Christmas this year. A month ago a lump the size of a golf ball appeared on my sixteen-month-old son's neck. It is something called a thyroglossal duct cyst, and it has to be taken out. Surgery is scheduled for this week.

Frankly, our personal situation threatens to supersede Christmas. How can I possibly think about the birth of another baby when someone is going to cut open my own? I dutifully await the Christ Child, and end up clasping my boy close to my chest instead—when he pauses from his giddy round of toddler mayhem long enough to let me.

Did Jesus squeal and race across the room the way my John does? Did He play hide-and-seek with His mother, draping wet clothes over His head while she did the wash? Was He obsessed with all vehicles equipped with wheels? Did He fling His head back and spread His arms wide with joy, shouting *"Trees!"* on a beautiful fall day?

Was the Baby born in Bethlehem *that* real?

Knowing that even straightforward surgery can go wrong, this Advent I am oh-so-intensely aware of how deeply I love my son. What a tremendous gift God has given me! And then, in the briefest moment of understanding, I'm struck with wonder: How could He stand giving me His *own* son too?

Heavenly Father, may the infant Christ, in all His humanity,
teach me the glory of Your unending love.
—JULIA ATTAWAY, DECEMBER 19, 1999

The Shepherd Speaks

The Lord is my shepherd....
—PSALM 23:1

*L*ord, I am so confused. My life seems like a series of accidents. I'm getting nowhere.

I am the shepherd. You are a lamb. It's not your job to know the way, but to follow Me. Through all the twists and turns, I am leading you in paths of righteousness. You'll see when you arrive.

But, Lord, I'm falling behind financially. Who's going to pay all these bills?

You shall not want. Your daily cup is running over. Remember when I fed you in the presence of your enemies? And the time I anointed your head with healing oil, when you were very ill? Trust Me, one day at a time.

But I get so weary, Lord, So very tired.

I know, and I want you to lie down in green pastures. I can restore your soul, if you will give Me a chance. But you continue to worry and work as if I were not here, and as if everything depended on you alone.

Doesn't it?

Not at all. I am leading you for My name's sake, not because you are so wonderful. My name is "The Good Shepherd" and I intend to keep My good name by caring for you. It's what I do.

But I'm getting older, God. Sometimes I wake in the night, thinking about dying.

Even when you walk through that dark valley, I will be there with you. I've already been through death, and I know the way. When you come out on the other side, it will be to dwell with Me in My house forever.

But I have so many regrets. Things I said and did that fill me with shame.

Just settle down. My goodness and mercy have been following you everywhere. I am healing those old wounds and cleaning up the messes you made. Leave the past—and the future—to Me. Pay attention to this day—it's the only one you have for sure.

Lord, as I come to the beginning of a new year—and a new millennium—
help me to go forward in faith, knowing that You,
the Lord of all the times, are leading me on.
—DANIEL SCHANTZ, DECEMBER 31, 1999

2000

Well, our computers didn't all crash, and our technological society survived the dawn of the year 2000. Not everything was so tranquil, however: a nationwide uprising overthrew Yugoslavian president Milosevic, and on Wall Street, wary investors sent stock prices plunging, signaling the beginning of the end of the Internet stock boom. In November, the closest US presidential election in decades (Bush vs. Gore) led to automatic recounts, litigation and a final resolution by the Supreme Court. And while our computers survived Y2K, they had a bit of real trouble with the "I love you" virus. And we lost one of the icons of our postwar world when Charles Schulz, the creator of "Peanuts," died.

Thriller fans pored over *Easy Prey* by John Sandford and *Indwelling* and *The Mark* by Tim LaHaye and Jerry B. Jenkins. Other best sellers included *Hot Six* by Janet Evanovich, *Winter Solstice* by Rosamunde Pilcher, *Drowning Ruth* by Christina Schwartz and Bill O'Reilly's *The O'Reilly Factor.* Moviegoers flocked to *Chocolat*, *Erin Brockovich*, *Gladiator*, *Traffic* and *Crouching Tiger, Hidden Dragon*, while we listened to "Beautiful Day" by U2, "I Try" by Macy Gray, "Cousin Depree" by Steely Dan, "Who Let the Dogs Out" by Baha

Men and "I Hope You Dance" by Lee Ann Womack. First-class postage went up again, to thirty-four cents an ounce.

Y2K seemed an occasion of anxiety for many. *Daily Guideposts* chose to look hopefully toward the new millennium and the twenty-first century (yes, we know they didn't really begin until 2001!). So we chose our theme from the Book of Revelation: "Behold, I Make All Things New." New to our family (now fifty-three strong) were Marci Alborghetti, who shared her encounter with melanoma in "Unlooked-for Blessings," Dave Franco and novelist Sharon Foster. Elizabeth Sherrill once again made "All Things New" in a monthly series, while Pam Kidd took us to Jerusalem to follow "The Way of the Cross." Mary Lou Carney shared the memories her mother had left as a legacy for her grandchildren. In Advent, Marilyn Morgan Helleberg shared the memorable Christmases of her life, and through the year, we made regular stops at Van Varner's Central Park West apartment for a story of God's presence in the big city.

Melody Bonnette of Mandeville, Louisiana, now a television personality and programmer, was a high school teacher when she came to *Daily Guideposts.* She brought us an educator's heart, a natural writer's skill and an appreciation for Creole culture, as in her January devotional.

Our second selection from 2000 comes from the masterly (and well-traveled) hand of Elizabeth Sherrill, who here tells us how, on a Normandy street, she discovered a new understanding of the Lord's Prayer.

Edward Grinnan of New York City came to *Guideposts* in 1988 and to *Daily Guideposts* in 1996. Since 1999, he has been *Guideposts'* editor-in-chief. Edward has a keen eye for the relationships that define and sustain us—with God, with our pets, with our family, friends and co-workers and, as in this devotional, with our mothers.

"First You Make a Roux"

My voice shalt thou hear in the morning, O Lord; in the
morning will I direct my prayer unto thee, and will look up.
—PSALM 5:3

Whenever I'm tempted to skip my morning prayer time, I think about making gumbo. A good seafood gumbo, chock-full of shrimp, crab meat, okra and bay leaf, is a favorite dish around South Louisiana where we live. Its rich, full flavor can be achieved in only one way. My mother told me the secret the first time I asked her how to make gumbo: "First you make a roux."

Like all Southern cooks, my mother knew that a rich, dark brown roux is the basis for a good pot of gumbo. And she also knew that a roux can't be hurried. Here's how you make it: Heat a little oil or lard in a heavy cast-iron skiller. Add an equal amount of flour, then stir slowly and constantly until the roux is a rich, dark brown color. It takes about an hour.

My early pots of gumbo reflect the impatience of my youth. My sister Sandi and I attempted to make our first pot of gumbo together. We stirred and stirred, waiting anxiously for the roux to turn the desired color. Our impatience got the best of us. We moved on to the next step and ended up with a gumbo that looked like chicken noodle soup. We telephoned our mom. "What did we do wrong?"

"First you make a roux," she said. "A dark brown roux. If you want a good gumbo, then you've got to take the time to make a good roux."

My prayer in the mornings is a lot like a roux, full of color. When I give it the time it deserves, it makes my day rich. It gives me the patience I need to teach 150 high school students each day. It gives me gratitude for a family that will be clamoring for dinner in the evening. The time I spend in prayer is the basis for my entire day.

So when the thought of the tasks ahead of me tempts me to skip my prayer time or end it too quickly, I always hear my mother's voice: "First you make a roux."

Loving Father, getting up early to talk with You is a small price to pay for peace I carry with me throughout the day.
—MELODY BONNETTE, JANUARY 21, 2000

Our Daily Bread

I have showed thee new things from this time....
—ISAIAH 48:6

ears ago, I was given a copy of the Lord's Prayer in French and got a new look at the phrase *Give us this day our daily bread*. To me there'd always been something unappealing in the word *daily*. Ho-hum, the same old thing, each day a repeat of the day before.

The French translate Jesus' words slightly differently: *Donne-nous aujourd'hia notre pain de ce jour*. "Give us today our bread for this day." For *this* day alone, I thought with new understanding. A day I've never lived before, when God's provision will be as unique as the unforeseeable demands of the next twenty-four hours.

Then I went to live in France and discovered how literal the phrase *bread for this day* actually is. From my apartment window in Normandy, it seemed to me that every passerby was carrying a long, crusty loaf: the laborer on his bicycle; the housewife with her mesh carryall; the schoolboy running his *baguette* along the iron railing. Bread for that day—and that day only, as I discovered when I tried to buy a supply ahead, as I'd always done at home, and next morning threw away some loaf-shaped rocks.

It was no hardship to buy bread fresh each day, for a bakery was always nearby. From almost every corner came the aroma of loaves hot from the oven.

Today's bread—what an apt image of God's provision! Given as we need it, close at hand, ever new.

Father, give me new bread for this new day.
—ELIZABETH SHERRILL, FEBRUARY 1, 2000

The Steak Knife

He giveth grace unto the lowly.

—PROVERBS 3:34

rowing up, I remember an inexpensive set of steak knives with plastic handles meant to look like wood. There was one bent one, its handle heat-warped by the dishwasher. By decree of some sort, Saturday night was steak night at our house, and you knew it by the fact that Mom set the table with the steak knives. Invariably, the bent one was at her place. Typical mother behavior, I always thought.

The number of table settings diminished through the years as my siblings grew up and moved out—I am the youngest—yet every Saturday, the same humble, deformed utensil would appear at Mom's place. When I teased her about always choosing the bent knife, she would say she felt sorry for it, the way I suppose she felt sorry for household spiders whom she'd scoop up in her hand and sneak outside before my father could dispatch them with a rolled-up section of the *Detroit Free Press*. It's true, Mom always loved the underdog.

Shortly before we had to move her into an Alzheimer's unit, a number of years after my father died, I showed up while she was eating dinner alone in that house once so full of children. It wasn't steak night, but, yes, at her place setting was the old bent-handled knife.

Typical mother behavior? Maybe. But Mom certainly wasn't egoless, far from it. She was proud, fiercely proud, of many things—her family, her children, her own sharp, restless, independent mind. She was known to brag a bit, that is true. But as I grew older I understood how hard my mother worked at practicing humility. She saw humility as a *spiritual* discipline, a redemptive one, a reminder of her role in God's world. After all, this was the woman who walked around on Good Friday with a sharp pebble in her shoe to remind her of Christ's suffering. No doubt that knife reminded her of something too: that even in our smallest, humblest choices we can honor God.

Teach me, God, a lesson in humility, a lesson in serving You.
—EDWARD GRINNAN, APRIL 7, 2000

2001

This was the year our world changed. Three-quarters of the way through the first year of the new millennium, hijackers rammed jet-liners into the twin towers of New York's World Trade Center and into the Pentagon. The other stories in the headlines that year seem to have disappeared from our minds: FBI agent Robert Hanssen, charged with spying for Russia for fifteen years; budgetary troubles attributed to a slowing economy and the Bush tax cut, the largest in twenty years; warnings from the National Academy of Science that global warming was on the rise.

The books we were reading included *A Day Late and a Dollar Short* by Terry McMillan, *1st to Die* by James Patterson, *A Common Life* by Jan Karon, *Chosen Prey* by John Sandford, *Black House* by Stephen King and Peter Straub, and biographies of a president—*John Adams* by David McCullough—and a racehorse—Laura Hillenbrand's *Seabiscuit*. At the theaters were *Ali*, *A Beautiful Mind*, *The Fellowship of the Ring*, *Monsters, Inc.* and *Shrek*. We listened to the *O Brother, Where Art Thou* soundtrack, "Fallin" by Alicia Keys, "Don't Let Me Be Lonely Tonight" by James Taylor, "Lady Marmalade" by Christina Aguilera, Lil' Kim, Mya and Pink and "Songs I Heard" by Harry Connick Jr. First-class postage held steady at thirty-four cents.

Daily Guideposts goes to press in July, so it was two years before we could speak to 9/11. This was our Silver Anniversary year, with fifty-three writers joining us in "Reaching Out," our twenty-fifth-anniversary theme. A plethora of special series included Elizabeth Sherrill's "When God Reaches Out...Through Other People," Isabel Wolseley's Papua-New Guinea travelogue, Eric Fellman's life-changing experiences in Africa, Kenneth Chafin's Holy Week series, Roberta Messner's search for restoration and renewal in "The Leaning Log," John Sherrill's look at "Rehab for the Heart," "A Weekend Away" with Van Varner, Mary Brown's experience with a dying neighbor, and Carol Knapp's look at the "Image in the Mirror" for Advent and Christmas, Marilyn Morgan King (formerly Marilyn Morgan Helleberg) and her new husband Robert together told us how they found "A Whole and Holy Love," and we welcomed a very different voice in Brian Doyle of Portland, Oregon.

Sharon Foster of Durham, North Carolina, was beginning her career as a novelist when she came to *Daily Guideposts*. Widowed as a young mother of two, she worked as a technical writer until she stepped out in faith to try her vocation as a storyteller. And what a storyteller she is, as you'll see in her 2001 devotional.

Pastor and professor Kenneth Chafin of Louisville, Kentucky, and Bellaire, Texas, shared his wisdom with our readers from 1995 until his death in 2001. And wisdom, hard earned through a life of service to church and community, is what we find in the Easter Monday devotional we present here.

Brian Doyle of Portland, Oregon, editor, essayist, memoirist and now novelist, is a writer's writer, a virtuoso with words who seems to feel their power in his bones. You'll see his magic at work in this tribute to his wife from his debut year.

Running Full Out

However, I consider my life worth nothing to me, if only I may
finish the race and complete the task the Lord Jesus has given
me—the task of testifying to the gospel of God's grace.
—ACTS 20:24 (NIV)

This morning, I woke up with Craig Virgin on my mind. For the past few months, off and on, I've thought about Craig.

Most of my childhood was spent in East St. Louis, Illinois. In high school, I participated in every activity I could think of and attended school sports events from football to track and field. It was at a track meet in 1973 that I first saw Craig.

It was cold that day, but I didn't feel the chill as I stood on the sidelines cheering for one or another of our school's track stars. Then Craig blazed by. I don't remember much about his appearance except that he was pale and had brown hair.

What I do remember clearly, more than twenty-five years later, is the elegance with which he ran the long-distance race—not his runner's gait, but his style. At one point, he began to dominate the race. I fell silent; all I could do was watch him. With little effort he seemed to pull away from the rest of the pack, first a few steps and then yards. That was when I realized that all the other spectators, who had been loudly cheering for their schools, were now silently watching Craig.

I don't recall whether a whisper sent his name through the crowd, or whether it was the PA announcer. I do remember that we all started cheering for Craig Virgin to pull ahead of the other runners by one complete circuit of the track, to lap the pack. Even though he was yards and yards ahead of them, Craig was running full out right up to the end, when he passed the rest of the group and crossed the finish line.

That day, I knew he was going to the Olympics. He did, three times. This morning I prayed that he is still running full out.

Dear God, help me to do the things you have set before me.
Give me strength and courage to run the race to win.
—SHARON FOSTER, MARCH 16, 2001

Meeting the Living Christ

Were not our hearts burning within us while he talked with us
on the road and opened the Scriptures to us?"
—LUKE 24:32 (NIV)

The minister of music had opened the service with a choir and orchestra rendition of the spiritual "The Angels Rolled the Stone Away," and everyone had joined in on the hallelujahs. After the invocation, the congregation sang the stirring hymn "Christ the Lord Is Risen Today." The sanctuary was filled with a sense of the presence of the living Christ.

But during a quiet interlude following the offering, I looked into the faces of the people gathered for worship and realized that a number of them weren't getting into the spirit of the service. They were preoccupied with some very heavy loads they were carrying. As their pastor, I knew what most of those loads were, and my heart ached for them.

I have the same feeling each time I read Luke's account of the two disciples from the village of Emmaus who were trudging home after Jesus' death with "their faces downcast." Though they had heard of the women's report, they had the same response as the apostles—it all seemed nonsense. As they walked and talked, Jesus joined them and asked what they were discussing. They were so involved in their own grief that they didn't recognize Him. They thought He didn't know what had happened, so they opened their hearts to Him. When they arrived at their village, they asked Him to share a meal with them, and that experience changed their lives.

To know the true joy of Easter, I must meet the living Christ in places other than church and on days other than Sunday. I may feel His presence in a thoughtful note when I'm blue or in the counsel of a wise friend when I need help in making a hard decision. But Easter won't really come for me until I know that every day, in all my comings and goings, the Christ of Easter is present in my life.

Lord, help me to celebrate Easter's victory in all of my life.
—KENNETH CHAFIN, APRIL 16, 2001

Numbers

Rejoice with the wife of thy youth . . .
be thou ravished always with her love.
—PROVERBS 5:18–19

First, there was the number I found affixed to the sole of her foot one summer night as she slept, her hair cascading, her face calm in repose, the faraway hollow ringing of a bay buoy in the night air, the ocean seething far below our room high in an old house: 75365, printed on a tiny slip of paper. After a moment I realized that it was the number of the person who had inspected the new sandals my wife had worn that day, but for an arresting instant I thought I had found her secret number, her mathematical name, the parade of numerals that had finally worked its way to the surface of her skin after many years.

I have since become a collector of her numbers. They come to me in bunches, herds, gaggles, most often when I am paying bills: Social Security number, license number, the identification number of her foster child in Egypt, account numbers.

I turn back to terser numbers: my wife's weight (105), her height (63 inches), the number of her teeth (32), her children (3). I think of what is innumerable about her: kindness; wit; courage; grace. I think of her sad numbers: beloved fathers dead too young (1), nephews dead before they could flower (1). I try to decide what single number would sum her up best.

But she is unaccountable in this fashion, and numbers slide off her like rain. No number catches her quick grin, the high-beam flash of her eyes, the leap of her mind, the utter absorption with which she rocks her children in the blue hours of the night, the grace of her hands, the elegance of her neck, the whip-crack of her anger, the calm mathematics of her limbs when she is asleep on a summer night, her hair cascading, the buoy bell silvering in the night, a sea breeze sifting through the screen door.

Dear Lord, thank You, with all my heart,
for love—and wonder.
—BRIAN DOYLE, JULY 9, 2001

2002

This year the US and Russia reached a landmark arms agreement to cut both countries' nuclear arsenals by up to two-thirds over the next ten years. The UN Security Council passed a unanimous resolution calling on Iraq to disarm or face "serious consequences." Kenneth L. Lay, chair of the bankrupt energy trader Enron, resigned, with the company under federal investigation for hiding debt and misrepresenting earnings. In response to the spate of corporate scandals, Bush signed a corporate reform bill.

The year's best sellers included *Journey Through Heartsongs* by Mattie J.T. Stepanek, *The Nanny Diaries* by Emma McLaughlin and Nicola Kraus, *The Shelters of Stone* by Jean M. Auel, *The Remnant* by Tim LaHaye and Jerry B. Jenkins, *The Lovely Bones* by Alice Sebold and *Nights in Rodanthe* by Nicholas Sparks. Big-screen offerings included *Harry Potter and the Chamber of Secrets*, *Lord of the Rings: The Two Towers*, *My Big Fat Greek Wedding*, *The Hours*, *Chicago* and *Gangs of New York*, while among the hit songs were "Don't Know Why" by

Norah Jones, "Hey Baby" by No Doubt, "Steve McQueen" by Sheryl Crow, "The Rising" by Bruce Springsteen and "Long Time Gone" by the Dixie Chicks. Prices were rising: a first-class stamp now cost thirty-seven cents.

In 2002, we asked our fifty-eight writers—including newcomers Fulton Oursler Jr., the recently retired editor-in-chief of *Guideposts,* Tim Williams and Billy Newman—to reflect on "Praying Together." Elizabeth Sherrill made the familiar words of the Lord's Prayer come alive, while Pam Kidd encouraged us to persevere in "The Practice of Prayer." Other special series included Eric Fellman on his and his wife Joy's twenty-fifth wedding anniversary, prayer at the four seasons with Roberta Rogers, a pilgrimage to the island of Iona with Marilyn Morgan King and her husband Robert, "A Worrier's Way to God" by Marci Alborghetti, a riveting Holy Week series by Roberta Messner, "A Grand Canyon Journey" with Rhoda Blecker, and Advent and Christmas with Rick Hamlin.

We've chosen one newcomer and two stalwarts to represent 2002. Fulton Oursler Jr., of Nyack, New York, has a double portion of writer/editor genes. His father was a longtime *Reader's Digest* editor and author of the megabest seller, *The Greatest Story Ever Told*; his mother, Grace Oursler, was the first editor of *Guideposts* magazine. Fulton himself, after a long career at the *Digest*, was editor-in-chief of *Guideposts* from 1992 to 1999. In his New Year's Day devotional, he combines his editor's eye for the fascinating fact with the spiritual insight of a man of prayer.

Roberta Messner is truly one of the most remarkable writers *Daily Guideposts* has ever had. An experienced nurse and hospital administrator, Roberta brings to her professional career and her writing a deep faith and compassion born of her own hardscrabble West Virginia upbringing and her lifelong battle with a genetic illness, neurofibromatosis, as in this Good Friday devotional.

No one in our *Daily Guideposts* family has had a more vivid sense of place than Van Varner. Over the years, millions of readers were introduced to the flavors of the Big Apple by his seemingly effortlessly crafted pieces, like this story about Christmas at a little coffee shop.

God's Good Time

This grace was given us in Christ Jesus
before the beginning of time.
—II TIMOTHY 1:9 (NIV)

*J*anuary 1, 2002. I look at the calendar and realize it is the first day of the second year of the third millennium. Every New Year's Day makes me think of the mysteries of time, the inexorable procession of this invisible force that rules our lives.

How much time has passed since time began? I wonder. Can our minds begin to grasp the strange things we have learned about the role time plays in the universe? I know the seeming exactitude of dates, hours and seconds is an illusion. Time, we now understand, is linked to space, and its measurement can be changed by velocity. Einstein and other great minds assure us that time is relative; under certain conditions of spaceflight, a traveler could return to earth only to find that his family and friends are long gone.

If time is one of the great puzzles God has given us, relativity is often seen as a threat to common sense. It seems to turn the world upside down. But is it any more startling or revolutionary than the principles our Lord brought to us during His brief time on earth? "Love your enemies." "If someone strikes you on the right cheek, turn to him the other also." "Unless a man is born again . . . ."

Jesus, Whose grace was given us before time began, spoke of the last days when earth's time will stop. And in the few seconds it took to write that sentence, I have had thoughts that span the entire arc of time. For an instant, the great puzzle seems clear. Everything—from the first nanosecond of time, through what we call the past, the present and all that is to come— happens at a pace no clock can measure. It happens in God's good time.

And in the new creation to come—in God's ever-present eternity—there will be no need for calendars.

Lord, Who made all time for us, help us
to make more time for You!
—FULTON OURSLER JR., JANUARY 1, 2002

A Word from the Cross

Then said Jesus, Father, forgive them;
for they know not what they do.
—LUKE 23:34

*M*y doctor had ordered a new pain patch that had amazing results. The fun-loving Roberta was back, full of pep and planning, and when I decided to go on a weekend shopping extravaganza, I asked my sister and a new friend to come along.

We had a great time, but on the dark, rainy drive home, my new patch fell off. Not realizing it would lessen its effectiveness, I secured the old (and very expensive) one to my arm with some adhesive tape. It wasn't long before I had a violent headache and was pulling off the side of the road. My sister took over the driving and I curled up in the backseat.

Soon I heard my friend remark to my sister, as if I wasn't there, "We're never going to get home at this rate. Does she get any worse than this? I don't know how you stand it." Her words hurt me in a place down deep that I didn't know existed. I'd planned our trip down to the tiniest detail, tiptoed to the hotel kitchenette each morning to brew a pot of coffee and brought a cup with a cinnamon roll to my friend's bedside, carried her packages when her arms got tired.

Then seemingly out of the blue, Jesus' words, spoken from the cross, flashed into my mind: "Father, forgive them; for they know not what they do." It was as if I were hearing them for the first time. Of course! My friend couldn't know what I was going through—she'd never been ill herself. And maybe she hadn't meant to be unkind but was just frustrated, or even scared.

When I got back to work, I printed that Scripture on an index card and taped it inside my desk drawer. It never fails to take my eyes back to the cross, to a forgiveness beyond my understanding.

What freedom there is, Lord, in Your model of
forgiveness in the midst of pain.
—ROBERTA MESSNER, MARCH 29, 2002

A City Christmas Past

*And that every tongue should confess that Jesus Christ is Lord,
to the glory of God the Father.*
—PHILIPPIANS 2:11

The hotel on my block, I'm sad to say, has taken on airs. There's a new canopy leading to the street, and blue window awnings, and elegantly uniformed doormen to maneuver the revolving door. The lobby, which has been expanded and paneled in oak and filled with luxurious furniture, is not the only thing that has been expanded: The rates have taken on airs too. But, for me, the sorriest thing is that, alas, they've gotten rid of the coffee shop and the jumbled crew who ran it.

It had the look of the thirties, with art for sale on the walls and, at this time of year, a pathetic little Christmas tree at the entrance. I had my dinner there once, maybe twice, a week, and I was often the only customer. I'd sit at the counter and they'd bring me dinner without asking: a cup of the soup du jour (the split pea was my favorite); toast, buttered; ham steak (usually) with potato and vegetable; rice pudding for dessert.

The boss was Greek, and as a rule he had his dinner and left for home, which meant that either Rumi or Roni, who exchanged shifts, was in charge. They were Muslim brothers, and they came from Pakistan. Eugene, the short-order cook from South Carolina, never took a vacation, and the smiling busboy, Rene, from Puerto Rico, spoke no English and resolutely spurned my efforts to teach him. Since I came from Kentucky, we were all regular New Yorkers.

I remembered each of them at Christmas with a little money tucked inside a Guideposts greeting card that carried the story of the birth of Jesus according to Luke. This to Rumi and Roni was nice, but to them Jesus was just a prophet. Every year I'd talk to them about Christ, the reason for the holiday, while they told me about the month of Ramadan, their days of atonement.

Well, nothing will be the same this year. I do wonder if Rumi and Roni will think again of Jesus, Jesus the Messiah.

I miss them all, Father. Please watch over them
with special care.
—VAN VARNER, DECEMBER 27, 2002

2003

In his 2003 State of the Union address, President George W. Bush announced that he was ready to attack Iraq even without a UN mandate. At the UN, US Secretary of State Colin Powell cited Iraq's weapons of mass destruction as an imminent threat to world security; the space shuttle *Columbia* exploded during re-entry in February, killing all seven astronauts aboard. In March, full-scale US military action against Iraq began.

The books we were reading included *The King of Torts* by John Grisham, *The Da Vinci Code* by Dan Brown, *To the Nines* by Janet Evanovich, *The Five People You Meet in Heaven* by Mitch Albom, *Blow Fly* by Patricia Cornwell, *The Savage Nation* by Michael Savage, Erik Larson's *The Devil in the White City* and *Lies (and the Lying Liars Who Tell Them)* by Al Franken. At the movies, we watched *Pirates of the Caribbean*, *The Lord of the Rings: The Return of the King*, *Finding Nemo*, *Mystic River*, *Cold Mountain* and *Seabiscuit*. The songs in the air included "Dance with My Father" by Luther Vandross, "Beautiful" by Christina Aguilera, "Cry Me a River" by Justin Timberlake, "Whenever I Say Your Name" by Sting and Mary J. Blige and "Next Big Thing" by Vince Gill. The cost of a first-class stamp held steady at thirty-seven cents.

The year 2003 was *Daily Guideposts'* first opportunity to respond to the wounds we had suffered on 9/11/2001 and the uncertainties that lay ahead. To keep our eye on the good things God continues to do for us, we chose "Everyday Blessings" as our theme. Our fifty-six writers included a crop of seven newbies: Harold Hostetler, a roving editor for *Guideposts* magazine; Julie Garmon, the daughter of Marion Bond West; Ted Nace, then Guideposts' director of ministries; Evelyn Bence of Arlington, Virginia; Ptolemy Tompkins, then a staff editor at *Guideposts* and *Angels on Earth* magazines; and Joshua Sundquist, then a student from Harrisonburg, Virginia.

Our ten series writers included Elizabeth Sherrill, Roberta Messner, Eric Fellman, Libbie Adams, John Sherrill, Rick Hamlin, Carol Knapp and Mary Brown. Daniel Schantz took us from Palm Sunday to Easter, while Shari Smyth kindled "A Light from the Manger."

Our three 2003 devotionals come from three reader favorites: Marilyn Morgan King, ever aware of the changing nuances in spiritual and physical lives, crafts a poignant vignette of a week in Kyoto with her husband Robert; Van Varner invites us to find the strength in our limitations by his honesty on facing his own; and Fay Angus introduces us to the unexpected wonder of a band of skunks.

Falling Blossoms

He hath made every thing beautiful in his time:
also he hath set the world in their heart....
—ECCLESIASTES 3:11

The night before my husband Robert and I left on our trip to Japan, we received a fax from the owner of Amherst House, where we were to stay during our week in Kyoto. "The weeping cherry tree in the backyard is in full bloom!" We'd tried to plan our trip to coincide with cherry blossom time, but that time varies from year to year, and the blossoms last only a very short while. So we were indeed fortunate to arrive at just this brief season of fullest blooming.

On our first day there, we walked the three-kilometer "philosopher's path" under an archway of gorgeous cherry trees, their boughs gracefully bent by hundreds of vivid pink blossoms. Everywhere we went during that week, we were awed by the beauty and lingering scent of these gorgeous flowering trees. But near the end of the week, it seemed as if the trees were raining blossoms. And by the day we left Kyoto, their branches were nearly bare. I thought, *How swiftly the pink blossoms fade into winter snow!* Suddenly, I was deeply aware of the shortness of human life, of my life! Then I remembered an admonition once given to me by a spiritual teacher: "What will you do with your remaining breaths?"

So what's my answer? I want to grow spiritually, enjoy my grand-children, savor Robert's companionship. But perhaps, as much as any-thing, I want to appreciate the simple things: the tang of fresh Texas grapefruit at breakfast, deer tracks in the new snow of our backyard, a surprise call from my son John, the satisfaction of a clean house and the scent of dinner cooking in my warm kitchen. I want to use my remaining breaths to be fully alive in each moment.

What will you do with your remaining breaths?

How precious is this life You have given me, Lord!
May gratitude grace each remaining breath.
—MARILYN MORGAN KING, APRIL 25, 2003

Survivors

And let us not be weary in well doing: for in due season
we shall reap, if we faint not.
—GALATIANS 6:9

Every year in June, my friend Joe invites me to a luncheon for stroke survivors at the Rusk Institute. Joe is one of them; so am I. We are both living with a communication impairment called aphasia, caused by brain damage from a stroke. Joe's stroke happened years before mine, and his condition is considerably worse, for understanding him when he speaks is far more difficult. He is an actor-director, and you will note that I say "is" because he continues as both. "How?" you might ask. I'm not sure, but through gestures, writing, facial expressions and just plain doggedness, he wins out. A play by Sam Shepard, directed by Joseph Chaikin, will be opening soon.

The luncheon was a wonderful affair. The people were as different as you could find—strokes are not choosy about whom they pick—but they were happy. They were proud of their progress, as was I, though I was in awe of what most of them had done with their affliction. I can speak, on occasion, and sometimes get my ideas across, but I am in difficulty if the idea is too complicated, and sometimes when it is simple, the words will not come. Fortunately, those whom I love bear with me. And the man I have taken as a model from the beginning is Joe. His doggedness is catching.

It was good being in a crowd where everybody understood. At one point I leaned over to the white-haired lady who sat next to me and said, "How long, eh, uh, eh"—I just happened on a moment of frustration when the words would not congeal. "How long..."

The lady cheerfully took out a pencil and wrote on a convenient pad, "That's okay, my friend, don't hurry. God has time to wait."

God has, Joe has, and I, thankfully, have time.

Thank You for using my aphasia, Father, to show me
so many things that are more important.
—VAN VARNER, JUNE 9, 2003

Dancing in the Dark

Praise his name in the dance....

—PSALM 149:3

*I*t was a paralyzing moment: A skunk had walked in through the patio door and was ambling its way across the kitchen. "Don't move," our daughter Katrelya whispered. "Stay quiet." I blanched, petrified at the thought of how we would cope if it let loose with its spray.

Slowly moving with the grace of a shadow, Katrelya went through the patio door, raced around the side of the house and then opened the back door so the skunk would have an exit. Sure enough, after crunching a dish of cat chow, Mr. Skunk raised his head, sniffed the air and lumbered out.

A family of skunks is raising their young in the woodpile across our fence, under a large Chinese elm in our neighbor's yard. We are becoming wise in the ways of skunks and are constantly amazed by their intelligence and amused by their unusual antics.

"Turn out the lights," I said to Katrelya on a late summer night as she came to the dining table to join me in a bedtime cup of tea. "Look—what's that moving about the bushes?" We both crept outside and peered into the darkness.

"It's skunks," she said. "Two huge skunks with their tails up and spread out like fans." Mesmerized, we watched. They were dancing, tumbling and chasing each other in what was probably a mating ritual as beautiful as an orchestrated ballet. Within moments they were gone, out of our range of vision.

"Wow," I mused, "I never thought skunks could be so graceful and lovely."

"Not only that," our daughter answered, "they make sweet pets too."

"Don't even think about it!" I gasped.

"De-scented?" she asked.

"Never!" I said.

In all our forty years of living in the foothills, close to wildlife, we had never seen the likes of this: skunks, the much maligned, dancing in the moonlight.

For the blessings of "all creatures, great and small,"
I give You thanks, dear Lord.
—FAY ANGUS, AUGUST 27, 2003

2004

In the aftermath of the invasion of Iraq, the US located no weapons of mass destruction. The summer Democratic convention nominated John Kerry for president while Republicans renominated President Bush, who won the November election. Lifestyle business magnate Martha Stewart was sentenced to five months in prison for obstruction of justice and lying to federal investigators.

Novels on the bookstore shelves included *The Last Juror* by John Grisham, *Glorious Appearing*, another installment in the *Left Behind* series by Tim LaHaye and Jerry B. Jenkins, *"R" Is for Ricochet* by Sue Grafton, *Northern Lights* by Nora Roberts and *Hour Game* by David Baldacci. The nonfiction shelves featured Pete Rose's *My Prison without Bars*, *Plan of Attack* by Bob Woodward, *Eats, Shoots and Leaves* by Lynne Truss, *Big Russ and Me* by Tim Russert and *My Life* by Bill Clinton. Movies out this year included *The Aviator*, *The Incredibles*, *Million Dollar Baby*, *Sideways* and *Spider-Man 2*. Among the song hits were "Daughters" by John Mayer, "Sunrise" by Norah Jones, "Here We Go Again" by Ray Charles and Norah Jones, "Code of Silence" by Bruce Springsteen and "Vertigo" by U2. We still paid thirty-seven cents for a first-class stamp.

In 2004, our *Daily Guideposts* theme was "The Things that Matter." We featured sixty writers, with special contributions from Elizabeth Sherrill on the hymns that have shaped her faith ("Then Sings My Soul"), Carol Kuykendall on "What Matters Most" to a family, and Roberta Messner ("Consider the Lilies") on God's provision for His children. A lot of travel was in store for us: In June Fred Bauer took us to the Costa Rican rainforest, while Van Varner asked us aboard for "A Voyage North," Brigitte Weeks invited us to join Habitat for Humanity in Central America for "A Time to Build" and Marilyn Morgan King took us on a pilgrimage to Wales. In Holy Week, we went "Back to Jerusalem" with Carol Knapp, and we spent Christmas with John Sherrill.

Joining us for the first time were Lucile Allen of Van, Texas, Patricia Pingry of Nashville, Tennessee, Philip Zaleski of Middlebury, Vermont, and Pamela Kennedy of Honolulu, Hawaii.

Scott Walker first came to us in 1991 as pastor of First Baptist Church in Charleston, South Carolina. Then after a long stint as pastor of First Baptist in Waco, Texas, Scott has moved to Macon, Georgia, where he is founding director of the Institute of Life Purpose at Mercer University. In the piece we present here, Scott shares the place of prayer in his own life.

Shari Smyth of Nashville, Tennessee, lived in upstate New York when she joined us in 1980. We've watched her as she and her husband Whitney raised their four children and became grandparents. Never afraid to share from the heart, Shari has the gift of expressing her faith with simplicity and serenity, as in her 2004 devotional about a trip to the attic.

It's not necessary to say much more about our third selection than that it's written by Elizabeth Sherrill. Here she shows how a hymn, a hymn writer and a blind old man helped set a teenager on the right path.

Building the Fire

The angel of the Lord appeared to him [Moses] in
a blazing fire from the midst of a bush....
—EXODUS 3:2 (NAS)

*E*ach spring I have a cord of oak firewood delivered to our house. It's stacked in our garage to cure and await the winter months and fireplace weather. There's nothing I love more than a chilly night, a blazing fire, a soft blanket and a good book.

Last night was such a night. Joyfully I carried the split oak logs to the fireplace, only to realize that I had nothing to start the fire with. Hearty oak does not burst into flame without the help of kindling, and I'd forgotten to fill the kindling box with pine scraps and wood shavings.

Over the years, I've discovered that developing my prayer life is much like building a fire in a fireplace. I need something to ignite the flame and get me started on my prayer journey. For me, devotional reading is kindling for my spirit.

On the table by my easy chair is the book I'm currently reading, along with my Bible and *Daily Guideposts*. The pages of these three books serve as my spiritual kindling every morning to spark a spirit of prayer. Reading them opens my mind to new thoughts and allows God's Spirit to speak to me.

All of us want to bask in the warmth of God's presence. But without spiritual kindling, it's difficult to build a fire within and keep it going. So don't neglect to fill your kindling box with good thoughts, interesting books and meaningful reflections. If you do, God will guide you by His light and fill you with His peace throughout the day.

Father, use my daily devotions to bring light
and warmth into my life.
—SCOTT WALKER, JANUARY 4, 2004

The Picture in the Attic

"Behold, I stand at the door and knock. If anyone hears
My voice and opens the door, I will come in to him
and dine with him, and he with Me."

—REVELATION 3:20 (NKJV)

Recently I was cleaning out my overflowing attic, a painful task for a pack rat like me. There were lampshades, picture frames, extension cords, chipped knickknacks. But the hardest to sort were the boxes of memories: letters, drawings, trophies and yearbooks that belonged to my husband Whitney and our kids. *I can't throw out any of these*, I thought. One box had my name on it; I spent an hour sifting through it, memories pouring over me. At the bottom was a tattered picture of Jesus knocking at the heart's door. The picture had hung upstairs in the childhood home where I first heard Him call me.

I was six or seven and alone in our living room, sitting on the floor, staring dreamily through a window at a bare tree and the blazing blue sky, when the picture edged into my daydreams: Jesus, standing on a doorstep, suffused in light, scarred hand raised to knock. A thought, clear and bright as the day, came into my mind: *Wouldn't you like to ask Jesus into your heart?*

With a child's matter-of-fact faith, I got up, knelt by the sofa and prayed a simple prayer I'd learned in Sunday school. Nothing changed, yet everything did.

Fifty years later, in the semidarkness of my attic, I was caught again by the picture of Jesus and held by the reality of His long-ago call. Through all the memories, through the turning of seasons, the passing of decades, the shifting of locations, through sickness and health, through pain and joy and failure, even when I let Him wait outside the door while I went about my everyday busyness, His love has been with me—my Lord, my Savior and my lifelong Friend.

Lord, no matter what else falls by the wayside, gets lost or thrown out, You and Your love are with me forever.
—SHARI SMYTH, MARCH 13, 2004

Amazing Grace

*Set your hope fully on the grace to be given you
when Jesus Christ is revealed.*
—1 PETER 1:13 (NIV)

He lived across the street from us as I was growing up, a blind, bedridden old man. I'd see him on rare occasions, being wheeled from the house to the car, to my young mind a picture of hopelessness.

How wrong I was! When I learned to type, Mr. Seldon hired me one afternoon a week after school to answer the letters that came from all over the country to this one-time organist and music teacher. His replies were long, personal and detailed—largely encouragement to former students.

I also helped him organize his huge collection of 78-rpm records. There was usually music playing when I arrived, often "Amazing Grace."

"I want to be just like the hymn's writer John Newton," he said once.

I was startled; he'd just finished telling me about Newton's life as a drunkard and a ship's captain in the slave trade. "I mean," he added, "like Newton after he lost his sight." Newton, he went on, had had a tremendous conversion and had become a minister and hymn writer. Then the man who wrote "I once was blind, but now I see" became blind.

Newton's spiritual sight, however, grew keener than ever as he went on preaching and writing hymns. When he reached his eighties, friends urged him to retire. "Do you know what he said?" Mr. Seldon asked. "He admitted that his eyesight was gone and his memory failing, but he said, 'I remember two things: I am a great sinner. And Jesus is a great Savior.'"

"Bad eyesight isn't such a disadvantage," Mr. Seldon said. "It helps us overlook the unimportant things and set our sights on the ones that matter."

Show me the things this day, Father, that matter to You.
—ELIZABETH SHERRILL, JUNE 1, 2004

2005

In Iran, former Teheran mayor Mahmoud Ahmadinejad, a hard-line conservative, won Iran's presidential election with 62 percent of the vote. In Britain, Prime Minister Tony Blair's Labour Party won its third successive election. At home, Hurricane Katrina devastated the Gulf Coast, leaving more than a thousand dead and millions homeless. And in Rome, John Paul II died after more than twenty-six years as pope.

Popular fiction included *The Closers* by Michael Connelly, *The Mermaid Chair* by Sue Monk Kidd, *The Historian* by Elizabeth Kostova, *Anansi Boys* by Neil Gaiman and *A Breath of Snow and Ashes* by Diana Gabaldon. On the nonfiction best-seller lists were *Blink* by Malcolm Gladwell, *The World Is Flat* by Thomas Friedman, *Teacher Man* by Frank McCourt and David McCullough's *1776*. On the screen, we watched *The Chronicles of Narnia: The Lion, the Witch, and the Wardrobe*, *Crash*, *Good Night, and Good Luck*, *Walk the Line* and the controversial *Brokeback Mountain*. We listened to "Sometimes You Can't Make It on Your Own" by U2, "Since U Been Gone" by Kelly Clarkson, "From the Bottom of My Heart" by Stevie Wonder, "This

Love" by Maroon 5 and "We Belong Together" by Maria Carey. It still cost us thirty-seven cents to mail a first-class letter.

Our theme for *Daily Guideposts 2005* was "Rejoicing in Hope." Sixty writers joined us, among whom were newcomers Debbie Macomber, one of America's all-time-best-selling writers, Sabra Ciancanelli, now the editor of OurPrayer.org, Pablo Diaz, Guideposts' director of ministries, Floridian Rebecca Kelly, and Karen Valentin of New York City.

Elizabeth Sherrill gave us "God Sightings" at the start of each month; Roberta Messner shared her experiences of God's little nudges; Marci Alborghetti faced the recurrence of her melanoma; Julia Attaway took us to the place where Easter truly begins—"At the Foot of the Cross"; Carol Kuykendall found God to be "A Very Present Help"; Marilyn Morgan King shared "The Mysterious Gift"; and Karen Barber showed us the "Simple Gifts" of Christmas.

Parenting as vocation and the family as a place of spiritual growth for both parents and children have been constant themes in Julia Attaway's devotionals. In the first of this year's selections, from her Holy Week series, Julia tells us how even the most difficult challenges of a mother's life can lead her to a deeper faith.

Life in the city sometimes has its unlooked-for—and unlikely— amenities. Rick Hamlin seem always able to find them, as in this year's celebration of his urban garden.

Like many members of our *Daily Guideposts* family, Gina Bridgeman of Scottsdale, Arizona—daughter of baseball player and broadcaster Joe Garagiola—came to us from the Guideposts Writers Workshop. A new mom when she joined us in 1990, we've watched her two children grow over the years and, as she shows us in this de- votional, how they all have lots of fun together.

The Silence of God

"Yes, Lord," she told him, "I believe that you are the Christ,
the Son of God, who was to come into the world."
—JOHN 11:27 (NIV)

I have prayed and prayed and prayed for things to get better. They haven't. Last night John's rage was so intense we had to pin him to the bed for three full hours. Today I am sore, both physically and emotionally. I don't understand what is going on. I don't know why God doesn't seem to be listening to my pleas.

Getting no response when I am pleading, crying on my knees to God is hard. Very hard. I wonder why God remains silent. He promised not to give me more than I could bear, but the combination of John's wretchedness, my misery and God's silence is very close to my definition of unbearable.

I stop to ponder what Scripture says about God's silence and turn to the story of Lazarus. While Lazarus lay dying, Martha did what she ought to do: She turned to Jesus. Jesus knew that Martha was worried and grieving; He knew her need for Him was real. Yet He did not come.

Martha did not know why, but she didn't wonder about it. Martha didn't second-guess herself, fearing she had not asked Jesus in the right way. Martha did not give in to fears that she had too little faith. She simply trusted that Jesus would respond in the way He deemed best. Her words to Him when He finally arrived were a clear declaration of faith: "Lord...if you had been here, my brother would not have died. But I know that even now God will give you whatever you ask" (John 11:21–22, NIV).

This gives me hope, and a model for prayer. Silence from God tells me I have to trust in God's will, which is manifested in God's time. If He wants me to wait and trust, that is what I must do.

Lord, You are king even of my anguish.
Let me serve You in and through it.
—JULIA ATTAWAY, MARCH 21, 2005

City Harvest

The earth bringeth forth fruit of herself; first the blade,
then the ear, after that the full corn in the ear.
—MARK 4:28

*A*ny real gardener would look with dismay at the pathetic plot of land I have claimed for my garden. A small patch of dirt in our apartment complex, abandoned by the professional gardener, surrounded by buildings, it gets little light and less love. One spring day on a whim, I planted some basil and tomato seedlings there. To my amazement they grew, and by summer I had four ripe tomatoes and enough basil for a small batch of pesto. Not bad.

The next year I planted some snapdragons and anemones and added parsley and mint to the basil and tomatoes. The mint came back the next spring of its own accord and the parsley did fine. In the fall I put down some tulip bulbs so I'd have a spring and summer garden. Sure enough, they popped up and flowered in April, just in time for Easter. That spring I put in some carrots, beans and zucchini. Alas, the beans never appeared and the carrots were no bigger than a thumbnail, but we cooked two zucchini one August night. And I added more tulips that fall, dreaming of a Rembrandt landscape on an eight-by-six plot of earth.

"For all your efforts, we have the most expensive tomatoes in all of New York City," my wife says. She's right. I could get something at the corner deli for a fraction of the price and effort. But these tomatoes (and parsley and mint and tulips) are mine. I have watched them survive attacks by rodents, insects, cats, heat waves and drought. It's my project with God. Out of a patch surrounded by concrete, a bit of nature flourishes. And I have never taken a tomato, tulip, carrot or zucchini for granted since.

Thank You, God, for Your bounty.
—RICK HAMLIN, AUGUST 6, 2005

Arizona Falls

Give thanks unto the Lord...
Remember his marvellous works....
—I CHRONICLES 16:8, 12

A sweltering Saturday morning in August seemed like a great time to visit one of Phoenix's newest attractions, the WaterWorks at Arizona Falls. It's a grand name for a simple idea: Use the water from the Arizona canal running throughout the city to create several cascading waterfalls and a hydro-generator to power homes.

The temperature was already 108 degrees, and my children Ross and Maria couldn't wait to bolt from the hot car and stand close to one of the big falls that drops water twenty feet into the canal below. The slightest breeze sent cool, wet sprays into their sweaty faces. Over the roar of the water, I could hear Maria's delighted squeals.

I closed my eyes and leaned closer to the railing, feeling the gentle mist on my face. How strange that only the week before we had been on vacation in San Diego—two cool, breezy weeks with the Pacific Ocean right outside our door. Yet on days when we visited the Balboa Park museums or Seaworld, we didn't even stick a toe in the water. Now, back in dry Arizona, we'd made a special trip to bask in the coolness of a man-made waterfall. How easily and quickly we had taken for granted God's fabulous gift of the ocean.

But it's not just the ocean. I have only to look around each day to see God's other gifts I take for granted. I live in a peaceful neighborhood, my family is healthy, my husband's job is secure—to name just a few. What that tells me is simple: When I'm talking to God, I need to say thank You more often.

Help me every day to truly see and enjoy all
You have given me, Lord. And thank You.
—GINA BRIDGEMAN, AUGUST 20, 2005

2006

Convicted of crimes against humanity by an Iraqi court, former dictator Saddam Hussein was hanged in Baghdad. Democrats gained control of both houses of Congress in the midterm elections. An eight-year federal study found that a low-fat diet does not decrease the risk of heart disease, cancer or stroke. Barbaro handily won the Kentucky Derby but succumbed to a serious injury he suffered in the Preakness.

Books people were talking about in 2006 included *The Hostage* by W.E.B. Griffin, *Cell* by Stephen King; *Gone* by Jonathan Kellerman, *Rise and Shine* by Anna Quindlen, *The Book of Fate* by Brad Melzer, *For One More Day* by Mitch Albom, *Marley and Me* by John Grogan, *The Audacity of Hope* by Barack Obama, *Godless* by Ann Coulter and *Dispatches from the Edge* by Anderson Cooper. We watched *Pirates of the Caribbean: Dead Man's Chest, Night at the Museum, Cars, The Da*

Vinci Code and *Happy Feet*. We listened to "Not Ready to Make Nice" by the Dixie Chicks, "For Once in My Life" by Tony Bennett and Stevie Wonder, "Dani California" by Red Hot Chili Peppers and "Heaven" by John Legend. First-class postage went up to thirty-nine cents.

This was *Daily Guideposts'* thirtieth anniversary, and we chose "Great Is Thy Faithfulness" as our theme. Ashley Johnson joined our family, an even sixty this year. To celebrate the occasion, we gave you a gift of "*Daily Guideposts* Classics," twelve bonus devotionals from such wonderful writers of years gone by as Norman Vincent Peale, Marjorie Holmes, Arthur Gordon, Eleanor Sass, Glenn Kittler and Catherine Marshall. And our regular series included a look at the "mustard seeds" of faith from Elizabeth Sherrill, "Turning Points" from Roberta Messner, "Grace Notes" by Pam Kidd, Holy Week with John Sherrill, Marion Bond West's powerful story of her prodigal son "The Hardest Good-bye," the moving "Comfort in Our Grief" by Marilyn Morgan King and "The Hidden Glory" of Christmas with Gail Thorell Schilling.

All three of our 2005 selections come from *Daily Guideposts* stalwarts: John Sherrill takes us to church for a bittersweet but still glorious Easter; Pam Kidd takes us to Africa for an unforgettable evening; and Marion Bond West tells us of her prodigal son, whose addictions have torn him and his mother apart.

Hallelujah Chorus

Sing...his praise in the congregation....
—PSALM 149:1

Easter morning! Hundreds of tulips and hyacinths, and the open trumpets of the Easter lilies spill down the steps from the altar of St. Mark's in Mt. Kisco, New York, proclaiming the gladness of renewal. The choir enters singing "Christ is risen!"

The choir...for forty-five years I've sung with them, but following a recent throat exam I've had to resign. This is my first Easter sitting with Tib in the congregation. My once-fellow choir members process past our pew in their robes. How I would love to be with them, today of all days!

I hastily correct myself. A church choir does not perform, our director never tired of reminding us; our singing was an offering "for the glory of God." Still, it was difficult not to think of the music as somehow on display before the congregation.

Here comes the moment when I'm most going to miss being in the choir! Every year on Easter Sunday, we lead the congregation in the "Hallelujah Chorus."

Now the organ launches into Handel's glorious music. The congregation stands. And suddenly my eyes fill with tears. Not because I'm not up front in the choir loft; these are tears of surprise and gladness. Suddenly I'm filled with gratitude precisely because I'm not up there with the trained voices and leaders. For the first time, I'm not following the bass line of a score. I'm experiencing the shared joy of Easter, joining in the voice of the whole people.

Everyone around me in the pews is facing some sadness or stress. "Hallelujah! Hallelujah!" we sing anyway. I glance at Samuel, whose son is in the Army, and Phyllis, facing surgery, and Bailey, so long out of work. "Hallelujah!" we sing. We are people who share a great secret; people who come together today to proclaim that Christ is risen. We are people of the Resurrection, and this Easter I am part of the worldwide chorus.

Christ is risen! Hallelujah! Hallelujah!
—JOHN SHERRILL, APRIL 16, 2006

A Gift of Peace

The fruit of the Spirit is love, joy, peace....
—GALATIANS 5:22

*M*hondoro is a tiny village in the southern African nation of Zimbabwe. On a country lane, the dust rises in the last light of day to create a golden halo around a woman who balances a huge yellow bucket on her head. She smiles as she sings a Shona lullaby to the baby bound to her side by a bright woven cloth.

For days, with the help of resources provided by generous donors, I've worked with a group to establish a home here for AIDS orphans. The going's been rough; there's a lot of sadness in a country where one third of the population is dying of AIDS.

Our host is taking us on a walk through the winter wheat fields. Night wraps around us. The stars pop out one by one. Off in the distance, the village cows are making their way home, the sweet sound of their bells floating through the air. There's no electricity in the region, but the stars are enough to light our way back to the little thatched-roofed hut where we'll have dinner.

The night air is cool, and I welcome the warmth of the glowing wood fire inside the hut. As I find a comfortable spot on the hard dirt floor, a man kneels before me with a pitcher, a bowl and a cloth. He pours warm water over my hands and then gently dries them.

From the iron pot bubbling on the fire, I'm served a plate of *sadza*, corn mush with freshly ground peanuts stirred in. I eat with my hands. In the darkness it's impossible to count the people who are gathered with us, but there are many. There's no conversation. There's no need to entertain each other; tranquility prevails.

I came to this country to offer what I could. But God, being a God of grace, decided to give me something back. In a little African hut, God gave me peace. Whenever the world gets me down, I'll remember this night.

Father, anything I dare to give is but a pittance
of what You give back to me.
—PAM KIDD, APRIL 28, 2006

Tough Love

"To the Lord I cry aloud, and he answers me from his holy hill."
—PSALM 3:4 (NIV)

We arrived back home from Dunklin at 10:30 PM.

Early the next morning, I went out to my son Jon's garden. I let water trickle over the flowers. Back inside, I opened the refrigerator and stared long and hard at the pimento cheese Jon had made.

I felt like stone—cold, emotionless, tearless. I went into his room. He'd made up his bed almost perfectly. As I stripped off the sheets, an invisible blow knocked me to the bed. I lay there, holding on to the pillows. *Jon. Oh, Jon. Jon!* I squeezed the pillows harder, burying my face in them.

Unexpectedly, pent-up tears erupted—the noisy kind with racking sobs. I wailed freely, loudly. Why couldn't an addict be all bad? All lying? All manipulative? All selfish? Why does he have to have deep rivers of sweetness?

My daughter Julie had been right when we talked earlier that morning: "You let yourself fall in love with him again."

The phone rang. "Hello?" I tried to sound okay.

"Mom, I'm in Macon. I had a five-hour wait in Jacksonville. I don't know what to do when I get to Atlanta."

Like a litter of puppies clinging to me, my mother-emotions begged to be acknowledged, but I answered coldly. "You had lots of answers at the interview." The curt words tasted nasty, bitter.

Despite his repeated calls, no one went to the bus station to pick him up. Our family stayed on the phone most of the day, trying to comfort each other. Around midnight he arrived at his twin brother's apartment. He'd walked about fifteen miles. Reluctantly, Jeremy had let him in.

Now the story of our beloved addict would start over. I had nothing left to give him but my prayers.

Because of Your great faithfulness, Father,
my prayers for Jon remain steadfast.
—MARION BOND WEST, JULY 22, 2006

2007

In the news this year, the US began its "surge" of some thirty thousand troops to Iraq to stem increasingly deadly attacks by insurgents and militias. California Democrat Nancy Pelosi became the first woman Speaker of the House. A UN panel found that Earth's climate and ecosystems were already being affected by the accumulation of greenhouse gases and suggested immediate action be taken.

The books we were reading included *Nineteen Minutes* by Jodi Picoult, *A Thousand Splendid Suns* by Khaled Hosseini, *Lean Mean Thirteen* by Janet Evanovich, *World without End* by Ken Follett, *Book of the Dead* by Patricia Cornwell, *Einstein* by Walter Isaacson, *The Reagan Diaries* by Ronald Reagan, Tony Dungy's *Quiet Strength*, *The Age of Turbulence* by Alan Greenspan and *Giving* by Bill Clinton. The theaters were showing a trio of sequels—*Pirates of the Caribbean: At World's End, Harry Potter and the Order of the Phoenix*, and *Spiderman 3*—as well as *Transformers* and *Ratatouille*. Music listeners preferred "Rehab" by Amy Winehouse, "What Goes Around... Comes Around" by Justin Timberlake, "One Week Last Summer" by Joni Mitchell, "Call Me Irresponsible" by Michael Bublé and "Stupid Boys" by Keith Urban. By May 14, a first class stamp cost forty-one cents.

"Strength for the Journey" was our theme for *Daily Guideposts* 2007. Rebecca Ondov and Wendy Willard joined fifty-seven returning writers, who brought us such memorable series as Elizabeth Sherrill's "Lessons from the Journey," Roberta Messner's "God-Finds," Isabel Wolseley's Antarctic journey to "The Beauty at the Bottom of the World," Edward Grinnan's "A Worried Man," Marilyn Morgan King's "Pain and Grace" and John Sherrill's "Eyes upon the Rail." We spent Holy Week with Roberta Rogers and Advent with Daniel Schantz.

Our 2007 devotionals all come from long-timers. Isabel Wolseley came to us as Isabel Champ way back in 1979. A longtime newspaper columnist in Syracuse, New York, just recently relocated to the Pacific Northwest, Isabel has written movingly—and humorously—about raising her family, about her Depression-era girlhood on the Kansas prairies, about coping with the rapid pace of change in our contemporary world and about her travels, as in this vignette of her voyage to Antarctica.

Our devotional by Phyllis Hobe tells the story of the young Phyllis' return home during the first great Northeastern blackout in 1965. By what we've always thought was more than a coincidence, it was the reading for July 2, 1977, the day that Phyllis died.

Our third devotional, by Fred Bauer, draws on Fred's journalist's eye for the perfect story to make a devotional point while teaching us something we probably didn't know.

Paradise Bay

*"Be silent before the Lord, all humanity, for he is
springing into action from his holy dwelling."*
—ZECHARIAH 2:13 (NLT)

This is our sixth day of sailing from the southernmost tip of South
America to Antarctica, but the first filled with spirit-lifting sunshine.
Today I'll step onto Antarctica itself, fulfilling the dream I've had
since childhood!

Zodiacs line up at the bottom of the ladder-gangplank. A dozen
of us clamber in, and we roar off in a blast of diesel odor, leaving V-like
wave troughs in our wake. As we approach our destination, centered in
a sea of icebergs, we drift slowly toward an ice pancake, its top claimed
by a pair of fat, whiskered seals—one asleep, the other slithering over
the edge.

The noise of the outboard is replaced by the strange nothingness of
total silence, broken only by faint ripples and the occasional *plip* of an
iceberg shifting position in its sea berth. We normally noisy passen-
gers become speechless, overwhelmed by the immeasurable vastness

that threads around, through, behind and beyond ice floes and white floating islands so high that they seem to hold up the sky.

The steep cliffs have no visible tops, only clouds. Fingers of fog, wispy as gossamer, caress and cling to rock walls. The air is pure and clear and as cold as an ice mask, chilling but comforting.

Will I ever again experience anything this awe-inspiring? On earth, no. In heaven, maybe. No wonder this spot is called "Paradise Bay."

Eventually our outboard cracks the silence and the spell. We wend our way back to our ship, which sits in the distance amid the ice, glinting in a sun whose rays turn some of the ice floes into crystal, some into pieces of sky.

> *"When I in awesome wonder, consider all the worlds Thy hands*
> *have made," I, like the hymn writer Carl G. Boberg,*
> *can only conclude, Father, "how great Thou art!"*
> —ISABEL WOLSELEY, JANUARY 26, 2007

A Light in the Darkness

Hold thou me up, and I shall be safe.
—PSALM 119:117

The summer of my final year of college, I worked in New York City, a real woman of the world, commuting by bus from my parents' house in New Jersey.

One evening on the way home from work, the bus came to a stop inside the Lincoln Tunnel. Traffic was at a complete standstill. Word got around: The entire region was in a blackout. "Better get comfortable," the driver said. "We aren't going anywhere for a good long while." At least my parents would know what was keeping me.

Finally we inched forward. After endless stops and starts, we emerged from the tunnel and slowly made our way to my neighborhood. With street lamps and traffic lights out, I strained my eyes to see as we approached my stop. The candy store on the corner was in darkness, and I dreaded the walk home alone.

I signaled the driver to stop. "Good night," he said. "You be careful." I stepped out into the pitch black, feeling more like a frightened child than a woman of the world. The bus pulled away. What was that light in the doorway of the candy store? A flashlight. Someone's there. "Dad!" He reached out and put his arms around me. I started to cry. "How did you know when I'd get here?" I asked.

"I didn't," Dad said. "But I would have waited all night." Then he took my hand, and with his flashlight to guide us, we walked home together.

My father let me know I was safe that night, Father,
the way I know I'm always safe with You.
—PHYLLIS HOBE, JULY 2, 2007

The Master's Hand

My brethren, count it all joy when you fall into various trials,
knowing that the testing of your faith produces patience.
—JAMES 1:2–3 (NKJV)

An eighty-year-old violin repairman named Etienne Vatelot lives in Paris. Yehudi Menuhin, Pablo Casals and Isaac Stern were just a few of his clients. Though Vatelot says that his hands are no longer steady enough to fine-tune instruments, his ear is still uncanny, able to diagnose problems—damaged wood, uneven fingerboards or the angle of a bridge, for example—for his trainees to fix.

I remember once visiting the shop of an old violin maker in New York City. He told me that two elements went into the making of a fine violin. The first was the wood. Fine instruments are made of north-side-of-the-mountain trees, he explained. "They have stood firm against winds and cold, and the bad weather has made them strong."

"And the second?" I asked.

"The touch of the master's hand," he answered with a smile.

People of faith, I've noticed, have often been seasoned by north-side-of-the-mountain trials and made stronger by their tests. And they, too, have been touched by the Master's hand.

Teach us Lord, not to ask for lighter loads,
But greater faith for steep and rocky roads.
—FRED BAUER, NOVEMBER 21, 2007

2008

In February, three men wearing ski masks stole four pieces of artwork from the Zurich Museum (a Cezanne, a Degas, a van Gogh, and a Monet with a combined worth of $163 million) in one of the largest art robberies in history. In March, the US government began to intervene in the US financial system to avoid a crisis. In November, Democratic Senator Barack Obama won the presidency over Republican Senator John McCain and became the first African American to be elected president, while Democrats gained control of both houses of Congress.

We were reading *Compulsion* by Jonathan Kellerman, *Unaccustomed Earth* by Jhumpa Lahiri, *Hold Tight* by Harlan Coben, *The Host* by Stephanie Meyer, *Devil Bones* by Kathy Reichs, *The Story of Edgar Sawtelle* by David Wroblewski, *Home* by Julie Andrews, *In Defense of Food* by Michael Pollan and *Outliers* by Malcolm Gladwell. We watched *The Dark Knight*, *Indiana Jones and the Kingdom of the Crystal Skull*, *Kung Fu Panda*, *Hancock*, *Mamma Mia!* and *WALL-E*, while we listened to "Viva La Vida" by Coldplay, "Chasing Pavements" by Adele, "I Dreamed There Was No War" by the Eagles, "Letter to Me" by Brad Paisley and "Stay" by Sugarland. In May, the price of a first-class stamp went up another penny, to forty-two cents.

Daily Guideposts 2008 took a look at some of the many ways we're "Surprised by God" each day. Some of our favorite series writers were back again (no surprise there!), including Elizabeth Sherrill ("Unexpected Blessings"), Marilyn Morgan King ("Letters to Tiny Toes"), two Robertas—Messner ("A Second Thank-You") and Rogers ("A Way through the Waves"), Carol Kuykendall ("Give Us This Day" on Carol and her husband Lynn's joint battle with cancer), Pam Kidd (an unforgettable trip to Zimbabwe to find "Bread for the Children"). Scott Walker ("To Abide with Him" in Holy Week) and Penney Schwab ("A Sign unto You" for Advent, introducing us to the Chrismon tree). Four new writers—Amanda Borozinski, Mary Ann O'Roark, Patricia Pusey and Jon Sweeney—joined our family, while the return of Richard Schneider after more than a quarter of a century brought our number to sixty-three.

The first of our 2008 devotionals comes from Carol Kuykendall, whom we met before in 1986. In the year before this devotional was written, Carol discovered that both she and her husband Lynn had cancer. In this devotional she confronts the lie that "cancer always wins" with the truth of God's promises.

Our second piece comes from our beloved Marilyn Morgan King. Here she shares her hopes and fears for a soon-to-be born grandchild she calls Tiny Toes.

Our third 2008 writer is also one of our most distinctive. Mark Collins, who teaches at the University of Pittsburgh, combines exuberant prose with an eye for the smallest detail and a dry sense of humor. Here a discarded apple draws him into a most moving prayer.

Believe

"Stop doubting and believe."
—JOHN 20:27 (NIV)

"Mom, you have to believe God!" my daughter Kendall told me emphatically when she stopped by our house one evening on her way home from work.

I knew she was right. I had just gotten the results from a biopsy, showing my ovarian cancer had spread to my lungs, confirming my Stage 4 status. I felt discouraged, and the lies had started seeping into my soul: Cancer always wins. You'll never get well. God doesn't hear your prayers. Ha! Your faith isn't even strong enough to get you through this.

I knew these were lies from the enemy of my faith. But they started growing bigger than God's promises as I allowed them to echo through my mind.

A few days later, Kendall walked into the house and plunked a wrapped package down on the kitchen counter. "This is to help you remember to believe God," she said. Inside was a wooden block with letters spelling out the word BELIEVE.

I placed it on a windowsill above the sink and was stunned to see, for the first time, that the word LIE is tucked right there in the middle of the word BE-LIE-VE.

Wow! What a powerful reminder that when I feel discouraged, I can focus on the LIE...or step back and BELIEVE God's truth, which is so much bigger: the truth that God knows our suffering and walks with us and will meet all our needs. Most of all, that He promises a future filled with hope, regardless of our circumstances.

Now, every time I wash my hands at the sink or rinse a dish or get a drink of water, I see that word BELIEVE...and I remember.

Father, help me focus on the truth of Your promises
instead of fixating on a lie.
—CAROL KUYKENDALL, MARCH 28, 2008

A Letter to Tiny Toes

Have peace one with another.

—MARK 9:50

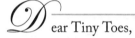ear Tiny Toes,

In just a few days you will enter this world. I can hardly wait to hold you in my arms, *ooh* and *ah* over you, and talk with your family about how much you look like your daddy or your Great Uncle Donal or whomever we project onto your little face.

As I wait for you, I've been thinking of some things I'd like you to know about this wild and tender world you're about to join. You'll find it's quite a beautiful place, with its sky-skimming mountains and twisty rivers; furry white rabbits and scary black bears; its shimmering aspens, yolk yellow in autumn; and its starry skies so full of mystery and hope.

It's also a world in which people are trying to love each other and live together in peace. But, my dearest little one, we are failing in that.

Perhaps someday you'll begin the search for peace within. It begins when you start collecting moments. You might set aside your sand bucket briefly to hear the whisper of the wind, or lay down your bat and ball long enough to enjoy a rainbow, or park your bike for a five-minute concert by the birds. Or maybe you'll be in your bed, looking out at the night sky, and everything will stop for an instant and you'll feel a quiet Presence near. Follow that Presence wherever it leads you, for this hurting world desperately needs those who can carry that kind of peace to men and women all over our planet.

As I hold my breath, awaiting your birth, the world holds its breath, awaiting peace.

Love always,
Grandma K.

Lord, may Tiny Toes and all of us find inner peace and become strong voices for peace in the world.
—MARILYN MORGAN KING, SEPTEMBER 22, 2008

The Apple and the Ants

He hath not dealt with us after our sins; nor rewarded us
according to our iniquities.

—PSALM 103:10

I walk with my eyes downward. I might look deep in thought,
but I'm usually considering whether my car is due for an oil change.

My downcast eyes recently discovered an abandoned apple covered
with ants. It was a fascinating lesson in nature—how a slew of insects
can act like a well-trained army to wrangle some sustenance for the
civilians back home.

It occurred to me, from my vantage point up high, that our little blue planet could resemble this apple: four and a half billion of us
skittering around the surface, working for our daily bread. I wonder
if we appear as disciplined and diligent, or if it looks as chaotic as it
sometimes feels.

I also wondered if there were ants down there looking up at me—
wondering, perhaps, what kind of being now controlled their fate. I
could casually kick the apple into the street, assuring a quick end to

their labors, or I could leave the apple where it was, allowing its temporary inhabitants to continue their important work.

I left the apple. In my heart, I'm praying that the One Who holds our little blue apple is more merciful than just. We have a bad history of, for instance, eating the wrong apple, yet we have been forgiven—again and again and again.

Lord, have mercy now and forever.
—MARK COLLINS, OCTOBER 7, 2008

2009

This year, in addition to our economic troubles, we worried about the H1N1 influenza strain, deemed a global pandemic. Scottish authorities freed the terminally ill Lockerbie bomber on compassionate grounds, letting the Libyan go home to die despite American pleas to show no mercy for the man responsible for the 1988 attack that killed 270 people. President Barack Obama was awarded the Nobel Peace Prize, while the major entertainment news was the death of Michael Jackson.

The books in our tote bags (and, increasingly, on our e-readers) included *Dead and Gone* by Charlaine Harris, *Gone Tomorrow* by Lee Child, *The Defector* by Daniel Silva, *The Girl Who Played with Fire* by Stieg Larsson, *South of Broad* by Pat Conroy, *The Lost Symbol* by Dan Brown, *The Yankee Years* by Joe Torre and Tom Verducci, *True Compass* by Edward M. Kennedy, and *Mitch Albom's* Have a Little Faith. The movie theaters were showing *Avatar* (in 3-D), *Harry*

Potter and the Half-Blood Prince, *2012*, *Up*, *The Twilight Saga: New Moon* and *Sherlock Holmes*. Hit tunes included "Single Ladies (Put a Ring on It)" by Beyoncé, "Make It Mine" by Jason Mraz, "Use Somebody" by Kings of Leon, "White Horse" by Taylor Swift and "Sweet Thing" by Keith Urban. In May the cost of a first-class stamp went up again, this time to forty-four cents.

"Living the Word" was the theme our fifty-eight writers tackled in *Daily Guideposts 2009*. Daniel Schantz led off with some of the ways "God Speaks" in our daily lives. Roberta Messner's midmonth series "With Eternity in View" shared some of the things living with a chronic disease had taught her. Also appearing monthly was Marilyn Morgan King's "A Time to Every Purpose" on Ecclesiastes. Elizabeth Sherrill's "Living the Word in Holy Week—and Beyond" added Ascension Day and Pentecost to our usual Palm Sunday to Easter series, while her husband John shared "Lessons from an Automobile." We traveled to post–Hurricane Katrina New Orleans with Brigitte Weeks and to the Mediterranean with Fred Bauer; Brock Kidd presided over our Christmas festivities ("Making Christmas").

We've had a hard time keeping our selections to three for 2009—it was a very rich year. We lead off with Alma Barkman, a mainstay of *Daily Guideposts* since 1996. Alma, a resident of Winnipeg, Manitoba, brings more than a splash of local color to her writing, as in this visit to the provincial agricultural fair.

We've already seen Edward Grinnan write movingly about his mother; here the *Guideposts* editor-in-chief introduces another lady in his life.

"As the father of five," says *Daily Guideposts* editor Andrew Attaway, "I'm never without material for devotionals. Here Andrew shares a lesson he learned from his eldest.

Publishing executive Brigitte Weeks of New York City, editor-in-chief of Guideposts Books from 1995 to 2003, is well known to readers for her love for knitting, a love that gave birth to Knit for Kids. In this devotional, she shows us how needles and yarn can help us knit together much more than a sweater.

Debbie Macomber is America's most popular romance novelist and has been reigning queen of the best-seller lists. But she's also a woman of profound faith, as she has shown in the devotionals she's contributed to *Daily Guideposts* since 2005—and especially in this one from 2009.

Hearing His Voice

"Incline your ear and come to Me. Listen,
that you may live...."
—ISAIAH 55:3 (NAS)

*E*very year I visit our provincial agricultural fair, held during spring break. I can usually count on taking some interesting photos: city kids encountering their first cow or horse or chicken, a little girl cuddling a lamb, or a boy proudly exhibiting his rabbit.

But the highlight of the fair for me is the horse competition. My heart always beats a little faster when I hear the hoofbeats of the Clydesdales in an eight-horse hitch, their harness gleaming, their feet in rhythm as they enter the arena. I marvel how their driver, his feet braced against the front of the wagon, skillfully handles eight reins at once, expertly maneuvering his team around the show ring.

Just prior to the competition, the announcer appeals to the crowd to be as quiet as possible and to listen as each driver gives commands to his two lead horses way out in front. Despite their massive size and strength, they obey his voice, flicking their ears backward to hear his every word as they lead the rest of the team through their paces.

Conflicting sounds easily distract me, so I find it amazing that regardless of how many teams are in the show ring at the same time, the lead horses of each team listen only to the commands of their own driver.

Lord, may the intrusion of other voices not interfere
with my obedience to You.
—ALMA BARKMAN, MARCH 25, 2009

Lessons from Millie

Ask now the beasts, and they shall teach thee.

—JOB 12:7

I'll never forget the moment I first laid eyes on Millie. Actually all I saw was her wet black nose poking out of a puppy kennel stacked on an airline luggage cart. My wife Julee and I lifted the kennel to the ground and opened the door. After some hesitation our little golden retriever emerged, looking both relieved and overwhelmed at the activity around her. *Millie*, I thought, *you have so much to learn, and I'll teach you.*

Well, wouldn't you know it, she's probably taught me as much as I've taught her. A few lessons from Millie:

- When you're happy, let the world know. For such a sweet, gentle dog, Millie has a monster bark. But she doesn't bark much except when she's happy. She reminds me that joy is contagious and there's no reason to keep it in.

- Hold your tail up. A trainer observed that Millie exhibits confidence by walking with her tail held high. "It makes other dogs feel relaxed around her." I should hold my head up when I walk down the street.

- Play, play, play. Learning to be a city dog is serious business. It takes a lot of concentration and practice. But don't forget to play like crazy whenever the opportunity presents itself.
- Be thankful. For every meal, every walk, every nap, every friend. With a nuzzle or a lick, Millie says "Thank you." I should remember to be grateful in all things too.
- Stay in the now! Millie greets each day as if it's the greatest adventure of her life. Her whole body wags at the prospect of a morning walk. For me, staying in the moment is the only way to experience God in my life. He is here now, in the moment, the greatest adventure life holds.

Thank You, God, for Millie and all the ways You use her to teach this old dog new lessons.
—EDWARD GRINNAN, JUNE 9, 2009

Out of My Depth

Give me understanding, and I shall live.
—PSALM 119:144

*O*ur daughter Elizabeth is back from a visit to her mother's cousin in Vermont, and in a few days she'll turn thirteen. It's been an exciting summer for Elizabeth; she spent July at math camp in Colorado, her longest stint on her own, and she'd barely gotten home when she was off to spend a week with Cousin Susan.

It's been a strange time for me. As our firstborn has grown, she's gone in directions where this math-challenged philosophy major has had trouble following her. But after her month in camp, I've given up entirely. Oh, I can parrot some of the formulas she's shared with me (she's taught her siblings a song with the refrain, "e to the pi i equals negative one"), but I have no real conception of what they mean. I can pick up a reference book and struggle through definitions of hyperbolic geometry and linear algebra, and I can listen attentively as she tries to explain set theory to me, but I know I'll never see them the way she does—as miracles of beauty and elegance.

For most of my life I've been a good learner, able to follow the threads of most conversations, whether in person or in books. But Elizabeth reminds me of my limitations, of just how far my abilities don't go. I need that reminder; I need to know that there's more in everything, not just math, than I can ever comprehend. When I'm reading a passage from the Scripture, I need to remember that no matter how well I know the definitions of the words on the page, I may be missing their meaning entirely. If I'm to look into the Word and come to know its Author, I can't rely on my own understanding. That's a good lesson to learn, no matter how young the teacher.

Lord, lead my daughter and me into all truth,
for You are Truth itself.
—ANDREW ATTAWAY, AUGUST 12, 2009

The Aran Sweater

That their hearts might be comforted,
being knit together in love....
—COLOSSIANS 2:2

y mother knew how to do Aran knitting, the unbelievably complicated combination of stitches that creates diamonds, knots and twists of yarn. Imagine twenty-four rows, each with different instructions and no margin of error—even one wrong stitch destroys the whole sequence. I've been knitting sweaters for Guideposts Knit for Kids for more than twelve years, but I've never even attempted the advanced Aran pattern. My good friend Ellen wrote a wonderful set of instructions, but I knew they were much too hard for me.

But somehow there was a connection in my heart between this craft and my mother, apparently effortlessly creating sweater after spectacular Aran sweater for every member of the family. How did she learn it? Why did she knit so faithfully for us all? There were no soft words of love from this difficult lady, but did we realize we were all wearing outward and visible signs of her inward and spiritual affection?

Every time I saw a fisherman's sweater in a catalog, I felt the tug of those memories. So one peaceful day last year I found myself on a porch, looking out toward the Blue Ridge Mountains of Virginia, with a sheet of instructions on my lap. I'd decided to attempt an Aran sweater for a child, unknown and far away. Four times I started, and four times I looked at the lopsided lines of stitches full of strange holes, unraveled the whole thing and started over.

It took me almost a week, but on the fifth attempt I managed a respectable little dark green sweater complete with diamonds and cables. As I held it in my hands, I felt I had finally, after many false starts, knitted a bond with my mother that I never achieved in her lifetime. Did she see my struggles and feel my woolen outreach? I think so.

Lord, with the work of my fingers may I weave together
memories of the past and hope for the future.
—BRIGITTE WEEKS, OCTOBER 16, 2009

A Gift of Tears

"For John baptized with water, but ... you will be
baptized with the Holy Spirit."
—ACTS 1:5 (NIV)

*S*omething strange has been happening to me in the past few years: I cry in church. For no reason that I can understand or explain, right in the middle of worship my eyes will cloud with tears. I blink furiously and take deep, even breaths to keep them at bay, but it rarely helps. My husband Wayne has gotten into the habit of carrying a handkerchief with him on Sunday morning. Apparently, he recognizes the signs now, because halfway through the service he tucks the hankie into my hand and gives my fingers a gentle squeeze.

If those tears in church weren't embarrassing enough, the same thing started happening during my morning prayer time. I'm most comfortable communicating with God in writing, but these days many of my prayers are smudged with tears. I was convinced that this was a side effect of menopause, but that didn't seem to affect anything other than my worship and prayer time.

My friend Wendy came to visit recently. I casually mentioned how easily the tears flowed when I communicated with God. She smiled knowingly. "That happens to me too."

"It does?"

She nodded. "Those tears are an indication that the Holy Spirit has touched me in some way."

I pondered her words for a long time and recognized the truth in them. My tears in church don't embarrass me any longer; they're my emotional response to the overwhelming love of God as He touches my heart with His Spirit.

Holy Spirit, sweep down over Your people and touch our hearts
that we might serve God. Amen.
—DEBBIE MACOMBER, NOVEMBER 15, 2009

2010

As we write this, 2010 is only about a quarter over, so we're going to leave the annual news roundup to you and forge ahead to telling you about this year's *Daily Guideposts*. Our theme for 2010—our thirty-fourth annual edition—was "The Gifts We Are Given." Among the gifts we were given for this year was Jeff Chu of Brooklyn, New York, who brought us a unique perspective as a pastor's grandson and a globetrotting editor-reporter. Also in our family of fifty-seven, Pam Kidd shared "Gifts from Above," the shadow of blindness prompted Marilyn Morgan King to reflect on "The Gift of Sight," Roberta Messner presented "Twelve Keys to the Giving Life," Isabel Wolseley drew on her own most difficult times to provide "Comfort for a Hurting Heart." Eric Fellman took a fresh look at Holy Week in "Encountering Jesus," while Elizabeth Sherrill discovered "Words from the Sea" and Marci Alborghetti looked toward Christmas for "The Greatest Gift of All." And most noticeably, we introduced a new page-a-day format to make *Daily Guideposts* more companionable than ever.

We've chosen Karen Valentin, Brian Doyle and Mary Lou Carney to represent 2010. Karen, a New Yorker and the author of *The Flavor of Our Hispanic Faith*, joined our family in 2005. She's started a family of her own since then, and you'll meet the new mother and her baby in this devotional.

As we've said before, we don't know anyone who can write like Brian Doyle. Put him in Hawaii, as in his 2010 devotional, and the result is truly amazing.

Mary Lou Carney of Chesterton, Indiana, has been a *Daily Guideposts* favorite since 1988. We've come to know her family, her friends and her colleagues at work, and from each we've gathered a practical, pithy life lesson—and, in this devotional, a taste of joy to get us through a busy day.

Becoming a Mother

Love ... always perseveres.
—I CORINTHIANS 13:6–7 (NIV)

Everything I'd read about labor and delivery promised ninety seconds of contractions maximum, with three to four minutes of relief in between. *I can handle that*, I thought. But the books lied, or else I missed the chapter about the labor-inducing drug that sent an army of torturers into my body every other minute for twenty hours! I was in shock from the intensity of the pain, and by the time I gave birth, I was completely exhausted.

Perhaps I was still in a delivery-room fog, but the tiny baby now wrapped like a burrito and surrounded by family didn't quite feel like mine. "Do you feel like a parent yet?" I asked my husband, hoping I wasn't the only one. Apparently I was.

Hours later, alone with the sleeping infant parked near my bed, everything still felt surreal. The baby was quiet and still like a doll, and had been asleep for hours. I needed sleep, too, but my body still hurt. I couldn't get comfortable, and every movement—no matter how small—was torture.

Finally I drifted off, but just as my dream began, the little burrito woke me up. His loud, urgent cry penetrated deep inside me to a place I'd never known. It made me sit up, gritting through the pain as I inched toward my son. I picked him up and cradled him close to my body, and to our mutual relief, the crying stopped. And during that peaceful moment, as I fed my little boy, I finally felt like a mother.

*Thank You, Lord, for the love that even in pain
can find a gift of joy.*
—KAREN VALENTIN, FEBRUARY 5, 2010

In Hawaii

Whatsoever Adam called every living creature,
that was the name thereof.

—GENESIS 2:19

I was recently in Hawaii, where I had dinner on the beach with a quiet, grinning man who started telling me about all the fish in the waters around us. After a while he just chanted the names of the fish, and we sat there by guttering candlelight, amazed at the artistry of the Creator. My friend sang to the fish for a long time and concluded by saying, "But the best to eat are *ahi, aku, au, awa, aweoweo, kala, kumu, moano, moilii, oio, ono, uhu, uku* and *uu*," at which point we ordered ahi.

Later I was standing in the sun in front of a tattered grocery store, holding fresh pineapples like prickly footballs, when a bird the size of a tent sailed over, and I gaped and said to a tiny man next to me, "Man! What was that?"

"That is *iwa*, the frigate bird, which you rarely see over this parking lot," he said, "though sometimes we do. And here I have seen *a*, the booby with the red feet, and *akikiki*, the creeper, and we also have here the *i'iwi* and *o'u'* and *nukupu*, who are also honeycreepers, and *pueo*, the little owl, and *io*, our Hawaiian hawk, and *ulili*, the little tattler who wanders, and our *o'o*, the honeyeater, and *elepaio*, the flycatcher, and *alala*, old man crow, and *huna kai*, the sanderling—her name means ocean foam. And we have *hoio*, the shearwater—he lives in caves by the sea—and *uau*, the petrel, and *aukuu*, the night heron, and *koloa*, he is our duck. And of course you know *nene*, the goose. There is one over there under the crown flower tree, see?"

"Yes, sir, I see. Thank you, thank you so much," I said, and he wandered off, smiling. I stood there for a long time, thinking that the language of the love of God comes in more colors and shapes and melodies than we could ever count.

Dear Lord, blessed are we beyond our wildest dreams.
—BRIAN DOYLE, JULY 16, 2010

The First Ice Cream Cone

And their joy was very great.

—NEHEMIAH 8:17 (NIV)

For the past several months, my four-year-old grandson Drake has been intrigued by the tall pile of ice cream that comes in a cone—and, of course, by all the licking involved. After years of cups and spoons, it seemed the time had come. So today, while his little brother was napping, I took him to the ice cream store.

Drake ordered in a loud, clear voice: "I want an ice cream cone. Not a cup." When the teenage girl behind the counter handed it to him, he gripped it firmly in one hand—too firmly, I feared. And his smile! It was literally ear-to-ear.

We sat down, and Drake began to lick...and lick. Only once did I have to take a lick to prevent the sticky white stream from dripping down his hand. (I did, however, have to get more napkins!)

Lick, lick. "This is good, Nina." *Lick, lick.* "I am a big boy, so I can have a cone." *Lick, lick.*

Finally his tongue scooped up the last of the towering frozen treat. Now came the cone itself. "I like this crunchy part." *Bite, bite.* Then a revelation: "Oh, Nina, there's more ice cream inside!" followed by giggles of delight.

One dollar and six cents and twenty minutes of my time. I drive home pondering the power of simplicity and the rejuvenating quality of joy.

Simplicity. Joy. I must remember how often those two are found together. Next time, I'll get a cone too.

Dear Jesus, keep me from making life—and contentment—more complicated than it needs to be. And thanks for ice cream!
—MARY LOU CARNEY, AUGUST 18, 2010

2011

Our 35th annual volume is dedicated to "Growing in Love." Our fifty-five writers explore the ways God uses people and the things that are part of their everyday lives to help them grow in love for their family and friends, their neighbors and co-workers, as they draw closer to Him. Special features include "A Path to Simplicity" by Roberta Messner, "To Say Good-Bye" by Pam Kidd, "Advice from Aunt Annie" by Penney Schwab, "Journey in the Dark" by Brigitte Weeks, "When the Heart Needs Healing" by Brock Kidd, "Letters from the Heart" by Marion Bond West and "Time on the River" by John Sherrill. Our Holy Week series is by Marilyn Morgan King, while Mary Brown gives us a special extended series for Advent and Christmas.

We hope you'll get your own copy of *Daily Guideposts 2011*, but to whet your appetite—and to round out our thirty-five years—we've included three 2011 devotionals. In the first, Penney Schwab of Kansas, who made her debut way back in 1979, explores a family tradition; Rick Hamlin returns with a tender tribute to his father; and a relative newcomer, Jeff Chu of Brooklyn, New York, introduces us to his most remarkable grandmother.

God's Autographs

And he had a Book of Remembrance drawn....
—MALACHI 3:16 (TLB)

Autograph books are nearly obsolete in this age of instant messaging, Twitter and cell phones. But family autograph books were common when my Aunt Annie was a girl. People wrote and collected brief notes and signatures to help them remember special moments and keep current on all the branches of the family tree.

Aunt Annie believed that God autographs the world in ways that remind us of Him. "God writes of His serenity in the moon-clad waters of Lake Erie," she wrote, "and of His majesty in Zion Canyon. His perfect design for the universe can be seen in a garden pansy, and fields of ripening wheat testify to His bountiful care for His children."

I've been making an extra effort to read God's autographs and I'm finding them everywhere. One day, shortly after my retirement, I missed my friends and wondered if they ever thought of me. During my walk that evening, a burst of golden monarch butterflies literally surrounded me, giving testimony to God's closeness. I saw God's hand in the kindness of those who prayed and called when my granddaughter Olivia suffered a concussion in a bicycle accident.

Best of all is the promise that I found in my Bible: "I will write my laws into their minds...and...put my laws in their hearts...." (Hebrews 10:16, TLB). Wow! God loves me so much that He will actually autograph my heart so I can learn His will and follow Him more closely.

Awesome God, thank You for surrounding us with
abundant reminders of Your love.
—PENNEY SCHWAB, APRIL 29, 2011

On the Beach

I have not run in vain, neither laboured in vain.
—PHILIPPIANS 2:16

$\mathcal{D}$ad found the perfect spot for himself this year on our beach vacation, at the end of the boardwalk in front of our two-week rental. He sat in his walker, his floppy hat on, a section of unread newspaper in his hands, and all those who passed by wished him good morning or stopped to chat. Some he knew; most were strangers, walkers and joggers doing the loop along the boardwalk. I went out to sit with him.

"They all like to touch the end," he said, speaking slowly, "either with their foot or their hand." It was as though they were in some race and had to touch the end of the old sun-bleached boardwalk for their mileage to count.

"What do you think about, sitting here?" I asked.

"Not much," he said. "There's too much to watch." There were the boats on the water, just visible over the sand; the waves rolling in; the swimmers treading out; and the runners and walkers marking their progress with the quick slap of a hand on the boardwalk wall.

I left Dad in his spot in the sun. He's lived a long, wonderful life and seemed especially glad to have his children and grandchildren close by for these two weeks. I watched him give the boardwalk a gentle tap as though he'd just completed a run. Then he stood up in his walker and came inside to join the family.

What a precious gift life is, Lord. Help me savor
every minute of it and every mile.
—RICK HAMLIN, AUGUST 23, 2011

Grandmother's Faith

Go ye therefore, and teach all nations. . . .
—MATTHEW 28:19

My grandmother was a woman of great faith. A missionary's daughter and a preacher's wife, she had been a Bible teacher in Hong Kong. After immigrating to the United States, she became a pillar of her church in San Francisco's Chinatown. You could find her there every Sunday, greeting the members of the congregation as they arrived, and every Wednesday, on her knees in prayer, seeking God's guidance for those same people.

During school breaks, I'd accompany my grandmother to the prayer meetings. Afterward, we'd shop for groceries, stopping at the produce stores, with their overflowing crates of verdant bok choy and boxes of red grapes spilling out onto the bustling sidewalks.

As I eyed the fat, round Asian pears—sweet and crisp, they're my favorite fruit to this day—my grandmother would hum hymns and choose oranges. There were always other old Chinese ladies around, and inevitably, she would initiate a conversation. Her typical opening line went something like this: "Do you believe in Jesus?"

At that, I would concentrate even harder on those Asian pears; I loved her, but didn't she realize how embarrassing she was? *How in the world*, I would think, *could she just start talking about Jesus like that?*

Looking back, I realize the proper question is *How could she not?*

I may quibble with her wording and her strategy, but I can't doubt her heart. My grandmother lived the great commission more than any other person I have ever known. She didn't have to get on a plane to go on a mission trip—she just had to go buy some oranges. And the good news she shared wasn't just meant for those old ladies next to her; it was also for me, as a lesson in what it really means to go and make disciples of all nations, starting at home.

Lord, wherever I am, give me the boldness to speak about You.
—JEFF CHU, NOVEMBER 23, 2011